CRIME SCENE INVESTIGATION
LABORATORY MANUAL

CRIME SCENE INVESTIGATION LABORATORY MANUAL

SECOND EDITION

MARILYN T. MILLER, Ed.D.

ELSEVIER

ACADEMIC PRESS
An imprint of Elsevier

Academic Press is an imprint of Elsevier
125 London Wall, London EC2Y 5AS, United Kingdom
525 B Street, Suite 1800, San Diego, CA 92101-4495, United States
50 Hampshire Street, 5th Floor, Cambridge, MA 02139, United States
The Boulevard, Langford Lane, Kidlington, Oxford OX5 1GB, United Kingdom

Notices
Knowledge and best practice in this field are constantly changing. As new research and experience broaden our understanding, changes in research methods, professional practices, or medical treatment may become necessary.

Practitioners and researchers must always rely on their own experience and knowledge in evaluating and using any information, methods, compounds, or experiments described herein. In using such information or methods they should be mindful of their own safety and the safety of others, including parties for whom they have a professional responsibility.

To the fullest extent of the law, neither the Publisher nor the authors, contributors, or editors, assume any liability for any injury and/or damage to persons or property as a matter of products liability, negligence or otherwise, or from any use or operation of any methods, products, instructions, or ideas contained in the material herein.

Library of Congress Cataloging-in-Publication Data
A catalog record for this book is available from the Library of Congress

British Library Cataloguing-in-Publication Data
A catalogue record for this book is available from the British Library

ISBN: 978-0-12-812845-9

For information on all Academic Press publications visit our website at https://www.elsevier.com/books-and-journals

Working together
to grow libraries in
developing countries

www.elsevier.com • www.bookaid.org

Publisher: Mica Haley
Acquisition Editor: Elizabeth Brown
Editorial Project Manager: Kathy Padilla
Production Project Manager: Poulouse Joseph
Designer: Matthew Limbert

Typeset by TNQ Books and Journals

Contents

SECTION V

CRIME SCENE RECONSTRUCTION

Foreword

I met Marilyn Miller in 1996. I was the lead attorney for defendant George Earl Goode, Jr., a former Marine, who had been convicted of two violent murders and was awaiting execution on death row. Soon after reading the file, it seemed clear to me that based on the science, he could not have been involved in the killings as the state alleged and the jury found. His lawyers at trial had not sufficiently challenged the forensic evidence and later admitted they had not previously cross-examined a blood-spatter expert who was the state's main witness. At that time, virtually no one challenged forensic evidence in North Carolina courts. Finding an expert to support such a challenge was considered almost impossible. The O. J. Simpson case, however, was recent then, and I watched the testimony of Dr. Henry Lee, known as the go-to expert for challenging crime scene evidence. I asked one of the Duke Law School students working on the Goode case with me to contact Dr. Lee for help on behalf of Mr. Goode. He referred us to Marilyn Miller. It was our lucky day.

At that time, Dr. Miller was assistant professor and program director for the Forensic Science Program at the School of Public Safety and Professional Studies at the University of New Haven in Connecticut. I would soon discover that Dr. Miller would help me (and my team) dissect the capital conviction of Mr. Goode. Since Mr. Goode was indigent and I was court appointed, there was little money to pay Dr. Miller for her services. That did not deter her. She came to North Carolina to look at the evidence. I watched as she meticulously pored over it, making superbly scripted, detailed notes to memorialize her findings. She later prepared an affidavit discussing those findings. She essentially confirmed the theory that the state had put forth false and misleading evidence at Mr. Goode's trial, through the testimony of an agent at the North Carolina State Bureau of Investigation, an agent who was later fired. I was certain that the agent's testimony and faulty forensic evidence had put Mr. Goode on death row, where he was waiting to be executed when I met him. With Dr. Miller on our team, I began feeling optimistic about saving Mr. Goode from the death chamber. Even before the National Academy of Sciences (NAS) Report "Strengthening Forensic Science in the United States: A Path Forward" came out in 2009, citing her first book as an authority in the section on bloodstain pattern analysis, it was clear that she knew the discipline inside and out and was interested in making sure that bad science should not be tolerated in any courtroom. Little did she know what a tough road it would be for the next decade to convince a court in North Carolina that Mr. Goode's death sentence had to be undone.

A short discussion about the background of Mr. Goode's case is important because it paved the way for similar cases built on bad science to be exposed. The state's forensic evidence was twofold: first, there was "invisible" blood on Mr. Goode's boot, found only by phenolphthalein testing, and second, even if a defendant did not have blood on him, that did not mean he was not involved in the stabbing of the two decedents, who were stabbed in total about 30 times.

In her affidavit, and in live testimony in 2004, Dr. Miller specifically stated that phenolphthalein, the presumptive test for blood, was not a confirmation or identification of blood. Although that seemed obvious to scientists, it was not for most judges, attorneys, laypersons, and jurors. Hearing the words "positive for the presence of blood" made them assume blood was present. It would take years to debunk that premise. Dr. Miller also testified that in Mr. Goode's case, the scene was so bloody that the killer would definitely have had blood on him, crushing the state's theory that a person could be involved in such a horrific stabbing and not have blood on him.

At the time of the hearing in 2004, Dr. Miller was an associate professor in the Department of Forensic Science at Virginia Commonwealth University. Once again, she came to North Carolina with little pay, a cold reception from the judge and district attorney, and faced a local community who supported keeping Mr. Goode on death row. Many experts would have politely reneged on their offer to help. As a lawyer for more than 26 years now, I can say unequivocally that I have never seen anything like it.

The state fought very hard to quash Dr. Miller and me in ways that neither of us ever experienced or expected. We were chastised for going against an establishment that had put forth this type of evidence for decades—evidence that both of us were convinced was faulty. With nothing to gain for herself, Dr. Miller stuck with the case, and with me and Mr. Goode, for many years. It was another 5 years before a courageous federal judge set aside the death sentence for Mr. Goode. Dr. Miller was the first person I called to tell the news. We were both in shock. I knew how important Dr. Miller's testimony was. Had it not been for her, Mr. Goode would still be awaiting execution.

Forensic evidence is now a hot topic, so the timing of Dr. Miller's new laboratory manual could not be more appropriate, and it is much needed. Folks in all walks of life are eager to learn about forensic science and how to correct the problems that were addressed in the NAS report that found a current system with "serious deficiencies."

When Dr. Miller coauthored her first book with Dr. Henry Lee, she wrote this in my copy in August 2001:

> This book was partially inspired by you. You are the "dream" defense attorney who knows how crime scene investigation, physical evidence, and forensic science are supposed to work in our criminal justice system. Thank you for giving me the inspiration and "keeping the faith" in the system.

How ironic to read those words, I thought. Besides feeling humbled by her words, I had actually grown tired of challenging the evidence without results. I was in fact losing faith in the system and wondered why I ever left working in a laboratory in New York City for 12 years to ultimately attend Georgetown law school in the mid-1980s. As a new lawyer then, I imagined the court system was fair and that "scientists" testified to the facts as scientists, not as advocates. In other words, they did their testing and reported the results: no hiding of evidence, no stretching the truth, no talk about invisible blood. That was my experience. It was not until I was cross-examining a state expert in a heroin case in the Washington, DC, superior court that I realized forensic scientists overstated their findings in some cases or stated results without any support. The eye-opener for me came during that case, when I asked the analyst if she was guessing that the evidence was heroin and after pausing for a moment, she stated: "It's an educated guess." From that day on, I knew not to take as gospel words from state experts as they opined about scientific results.

Dr. Miller has been a determined advocate for making sure science is not twisted in a classroom or a courtroom to merely advance the wishes of a party to a lawsuit. She is an advocate for the evidence, plain and simple. I am thrilled to know that the next generation of students will have easy access to such comprehensive materials. Dr. Miller's laboratory manual teaches the importance of implementing and strengthening rigorous scientific procedures to produce valid results because, simply stated, that is good science.

Because of its hands-on quality, I am certain this manual will become a go-to authority for everyone taking courses in forensics. They will learn from actual crime scene investigations what will enable them to decisively examine and solve problems. They will learn the importance of proper documentation and how contamination plagues the forensics community and what can be done to avoid it. They will gain the principal knowledge necessary for most scientific crime scene investigation courses or training.

Dr. Miller's extensive experience as a forensic chemist, an instructor, a lecturer, a professor, an author, and a winner of many awards in her field makes her uniquely qualified to write this manual. I look forward to seeing it on the desks of everyone interested in advocating for the evidence.

Diane M.B. Savage, J.D.
President, North Carolina Attorneys for Science and Technology (NCAST)

Preface and Introduction

Over the last 15 years, colleges and universities and even high school curricula across the world have experienced exponential growth of forensic science and criminal justice programs. All of these programs include at least one crime scene investigation course, and an essential part of the growth of these programs has been the demand for textbooks and materials. Additionally, the demand and need for a laboratory manual of practical, tactile, crime scene relevant exercises has been strong. Recently, large numbers of new publications or texts about crime scene investigations have arrived on the market, but most of them lack the necessary hands-on exercises supplied here. It has been up to instructors or training officers to develop their own exercises. This laboratory manual will meet and exceed this demand for high school students, college and university programs, and even for training purposes for law enforcement. As the need for scientific applications at the crime scene increase, a manual such as this one will be in high demand.

PURPOSE/SUMMARY OF THE MANUAL

This laboratory manual will provide laboratory or application exercises for users that will supplement any textbook that may be used by *any* crime scene course offered in high school, in college, and even for law enforcement training. Crime scene investigation requires practice and hands-on learning experiences. This manual offers a large number of proven exercises to provide hands-on learning that will correspond to the main topics and basics of crime scene investigation. There are only a limited number of laboratory manuals (fewer than a dozen) to supplement the textbooks that are published on crime scene investigation. What is unique about this manual is that it will allow a student to apply the basic science necessary for each exercise. Based on my experience over 30 years as a crime scene investigator/forensic scientist and a college professor, I have amassed a huge amount of practical application exercises that work nicely in a classroom or training situation. The manual is intended to supplement any good crime scene investigation textbook, but it can stand alone for great, hands-on learning need for a science-based crime scene investigation.

COVERAGE AND APPROACH/TABLE OF CONTENTS

The table of contents is arranged by topic, and within each exercise are learning objectives for the exercise. There will be many parts or sections for the exercises. Each exercise will have material from actual crime scene investigations that will engage the student to critically analyze and solve problems. Discussion questions and answers for each exercise are also included. This second edition also includes a glossary of common terms.

The exercises cover most of the basic concepts and foundational knowledge necessary for most scientific crime scene investigation courses or training sessions. Included in the manual is the use of 3-D laser scanners for crime scene documentation and investigation. These scanning lasers are finding their way into the larger law enforcement agencies, and for that reason they are covered briefly. There is widespread use of computer-aided drawing programs for sketching crime scenes. These programs are widely varied and constantly evolving, and as such, they are not part of this manual. For this revised edition, the exercises will still be technically correct and suited for high school seniors as part of a forensic science course, any college-level criminal justice or forensic science curriculum, and especially for law enforcement training needs. The exercises have been vetted and tested based on previous use in existing courses taught by an experienced educator and former crime scene investigator/forensic scientist. All current market manuals in this area are written by law enforcement personnel with nonexistent or limited experimental design and sometimes do not work well in an academic setting. Conversely, some existing manuals are written by academics who have no actual crime scene experience and therefore lack credibility in law enforcement training courses. This manual will satisfy both stakeholder groups.

Acknowledgments

How does a crime scene investigator get practice before being faced with a real case? How can I give a student a "real-life" experience in a classroom?

This laboratory manual that attempts to address these questions represents a project that I have worked on for the better part of 23 years as an educator and 14 years as a forensic scientist responding to crime scenes.

Many thanks to Virginia Commonwealth University (VCU) for having the foresight to establish the best forensic science program in the United States—okay…the world. The graduate and undergraduate forensic science programs in the College of Humanities and Sciences at VCU are both FEPAC accredited, which is a significant accomplishment. Thanks to VCU, the College of Humanities and Sciences, and the Department of Forensic Science. The amazing original artwork was prepared by Allyson Parrott.

Finally, a thank you to the thousands of former and current students, my kids, who are the reason I really like going to work each day and want to do the best in job I can.

CRIME SCENE INVESTIGATION: SCIENTIFIC METHODOLOGY AND PHYSICAL EVIDENCE

Exercise A

Defining a Crime Scene

Learning Objectives

- To identify the various definitions for crime scenes to assist the investigator.
- To understand the limitations of the scene definitions as a means of describing a crime scene and its evidence.

The "site of criminal activity" is the traditional definition of a crime scene. This definition is too broad but allows the crime scene investigator to anticipate the presence of physical evidence. However it offers no assistance or help in describing what types of evidence might be present. A definition based on the types of physical evidence anticipated can be constraining in that it may inadvertently cause an investigator to miss crucial, unanticipated evidence. Definitions of this type include defining a scene based on evidence size (macroscopic or microscopic), type of crime (shooting, stabbing, beating, sexual assault, etc.), or type of evidence (blood, drugs, explosives, etc.). Crime scenes can also be defined based on location (inside, outside, underwater, in cars, etc.). This offers clues to accessibility but offers no assistance with physical evidence anticipation. The determination of sequence can often be useful as a definition, especially for investigative or reconstruction purposes. The identification of a primary or secondary scene is not related to importance but is simply a means for identifying which scene occurred first (primary) and then the subsequent scenes (secondary).

All these definitions can be used for investigations of a wide variety of crime scenes. They can assist with anticipation of supplies or equipment that might be needed at the scene. They give clues to assist the investigators in their preparations for specific types of "difficult" evidence that may be present. The practical use of the definitions is that a thoughtful, science-based crime scene investigator will need to be prepared to apply all definitions to any possible crime scene.

LABORATORY EXERCISE

This exercise will provide you with an image of a crime scene. You will be asked to define the crime scene based on the various definitions. There will be advantages and disadvantages to each definition as it is applied to the crime scene illustrated. See Fig. A.1.

FIGURE A.1   Crime scene to define.

Laboratory Data Sheet

Definition Type	Rationale for Definition	Advantages for Definition	Disadvantages for Definition
Traditional			
Physical evidence types present			
Physical evidence sizes present			
Physical evidence type of crime			
Location			
Sequence			

I. CRIME SCENE INVESTIGATION: SCIENTIFIC METHODOLOGY AND PHYSICAL EVIDENCE

DISCUSSION QUESTIONS

1. Was it possible to define this crime scene using all the definitions? If not, which ones were you able to use?

2. What is the value for having many different definitions for application to crime scene investigations?

Exercise B

Physical Evidence at the Crime Scenes

Learning Objectives

- To identify the category of evidence found at the crime scene based on its composition or makeup.
- To identity and use the information that can be determined from the scene evidence.

Anything can be physical evidence. It is the debris of criminal activity. While there is considerable overlap in the identification of evidence, it can be categorized into the following broad categories based on its origin, composition, or method of creation:

a. *Biological evidence*—Any evidence derived from a living item. This includes physiological fluids, plants, and some biological pathogens.
b. *Chemical evidence*—Any evidence with identifiable chemicals present.
c. *Patterned evidence*—Any evidence with a pattern or a predictable pattern of appearance.
d. *Trace evidence*—Any evidence of such a small size so as to be overlooked or not recognized.

In addition to identifying the types of physical evidence found at a crime scene, it is possible to obtain valuable investigative information from the analysis of the item of physical evidence. The types of information that can be obtained from the analysis of physical evidence include the following:

- *Determination of corpus delicti*—The evidence is used to determine if a crime has taken place. For example, a broken window may or may not signify a burglary.
- *Modus operandi identification*—A criminal's repeat behavior. Repeated methods of entry—for example through roof accesses—are a clue to the criminal's identity.
- *Association or linkage/the Locard's Exchange Principle*—The transfer of evidence by contact; see Exercise C.

Crime Scene Investigation Laboratory Manual, Second Edition
http://dx.doi.org/10.1016/B978-0-12-812845-9.00002-9

- *Disproving/supporting victim/suspect/witness statements*—The evidence may or may not support what these groups say. For example, an eyewitness may say that a vehicle involved in a hit and run was red, but the paint chips at the scene are blue.
- *Identification of suspects/victims/crime scene location*—Fingerprints and even DNA can be used to identify who was present at a crime scene.
- *Provide for investigative leads for detectives*—The use of the physical evidence to give information to detectives, which will assist them in locating victims and suspects. An example is determining the make, model, and year of the vehicle involved in a hit and run that left paint chips at the crime scene.

LABORATORY EXERCISE

For this exercise you will be given a crime scene to investigate from the viewpoint of the type of evidence that is present. Identify at least five different types of physical evidence present, a second category if possible, and, finally, the information that can be obtained from the collection and analysis of the piece of evidence as it relates to the crime scene investigation.

The crime scene you are investigating is shown in Fig. B.1. Identify the type of evidence category (and second category if possible) and the information that could be provided by the evidence.

FIGURE B.1   Crime scene.

Laboratory Data Sheet

Identification of Evidence Found in the Crime Scene	Category of Evidence Found	Second Category (If Possible)	Information to be Obtained From Evidence

DISCUSSION QUESTIONS

1. Were there several points at which the evidence found at the crime scene fell into more than one category? If you were a crime scene investigator, how would these different categories help you do your job at the scene?

2. Should crime scene investigators function as detectives too? Why or why not?

3. Can the information collected from the physical evidence be obtained only in the crime lab or can it also be accomplished at the crime scene? Give an example.

Exercise C

A Practical Exercise of the Locard Exchange Principle

Learning Objectives

- To classify evidence as corroborative (alibi), associative (linking), or individualizable.
- To understand the Locard's Exchange Principle by applying it to a crime scene and the physical evidence present.

The Locard's Exchange Principle is the foundation for the use of physical evidence in a criminal investigation. The principle states that whenever two objects are in contact, there will always be a mutual exchange of matter between them. For example: Your cat transfers hairs to you when you pet it; this is *direct transfer*. Alternately, you sit in a chair and the cat hair is transferred from you from you to the chair. The cat never sat in the chair; this is *indirect transfer* (see Fig. C.1).

Crime Scene Investigation Laboratory Manual, Second Edition
http://dx.doi.org/10.1016/B978-0-12-812845-9.00003-0

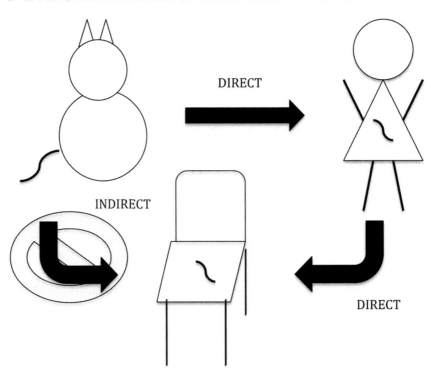

FIGURE C.1   Mechanisms of transfer.

LABORATORY EXERCISE

This exercise will be used to develop a better understanding of the Locard's Exchange Principle and the nature and value of physical evidence in the investigation of criminal activity. The student will develop a two-page description of an incident or criminal investigation. It can be any type of crime: murder, sexual assault, armed robbery, white-collar crime, etc. In the investigation scenario, the student will focus on the physical evidence and how it is used in the investigation.

Use your imagination for the crime and the investigation. Identify a minimum of 6 and a maximum of 10 items of physical evidence and their proper use in the case scenario. The physical evidence should be grouped into the following classifications:

- *Corroborative or alibi evidence*—This evidence will help establish the veracity of a victim, suspect, or witness.
- *Associative or linking evidence*—This evidence will be used to link a victim to a suspect, a victim or a suspect to a crime scene, or other possible linkages.
- *Individualizable evidence*—This is evidence that will allow for the determination of the origin of the evidence. This type of evidence unambiguously links a suspect to a victim to a crime scene and all permutations.

The case scenario should be designed so that the incorporation of the physical evidence is believable and easily incorporated into the totality of the case. Please attach the following physical evidence itemized list as an appendix to the paper.

Laboratory Data Sheet

Physical Evidence: Itemized List.

Item of Physical Evidence Evidence Classification.

1. _____ _____

2. _____ _____

3. _____ _____

4. _____ _____

5. _____ _____

6. _____ _____

7. _____ _____

8. _____ _____

9. _____ _____

10. _____ _____

DISCUSSION QUESTIONS

1. Were there pieces of physical evidence that fell into more than one classification of evidence? If so, which ones?

2. What were the advantages and/or disadvantages of having more than one classification for the physical evidence?

INITIAL RESPONSIBILITIES AND BEGINNING SCIENTIFIC CRIME SCENE INVESTIGATION

Exercise D

First Responders at the Crime Scene

Learning Objectives

- To identify the duties and common problems of the first responders at a crime scene.
- To understand the value of the first responders to the crime scene investigation.

The first responders to a crime scene are usually law enforcement officers, emergency medical personnel, or fire department personnel. Their actions at the scene can help or hurt the foundation for the successful resolution of the crime based on the physical evidence present at the scene. These first responding officers are the only people to view the crime scene in its original condition. They are also, in many cases, some of the individuals who may, through the course of "doing their job," inadvertently change or alter the crime scene from its original condition. They must do their job, but they must always keep in mind that they will begin or interrupt the process of linking the crime scene to the victim, the witnesses, and, ultimately, the suspect. Any disruption of the crime scene by the responders may prevent the link and break the Locard's Exchange Principle!

The first responders' duties are as follows:
1. Assist the victim.
2. Arrest the suspect and search for or apprehend any suspect still on the scene or in the vicinity.
3. Detain witnesses; witnesses who have valuable information about the crime scene will need to be interviewed by detectives.
4. Protect the crime scene and begin the crime scene protection measures. Consider any POEs (points of entry or exit); if any potential physical evidence—especially transient evidence or patterned evidence—is likely to be lost, contaminated, or altered from its original condition, then it should be recorded and protected.
5. All actions, observations, or changes to the crime scene by the first responders will be reported to the crime scene investigator. A reasonable attempt to avoid disturbing the scene in any way should be the guide that most first responders follow.

Any crime scene investigator and, hopefully, the first responders must have an open and objective mind when approaching the crime scene. Mistakes made at this beginning step could jeopardize the entire investigation. It is for this reason that first responders must thoroughly document their observations of and actions at the crime scene. Documentation, minimally in the form of recording notes or in combination with sketches, is especially well suited for this purpose. A good guideline for a first responder's documentation is to answer the questions: Who? What? When? Where? and How? Some specific examples include observations about vehicles parked at or vehicles leaving the crime scene vicinity, medications located next to the victim, any persons present at or who have left the scene, any disturbances or objects out of place, whether any dated materials (newspapers, letters, or notes) are observed adjacent to the victim, and whether any objects have been touched or moved. If careful protection, documentation, and preservation measures are performed by the first responders, then the "original" condition of the crime scene will be known and nothing will be lost or contaminated.

LABORATORY EXERCISE

For this lab exercise, a sample crime scene will be shown (see Fig. D.1). Answer the following questions.

FIGURE D.1 Overview of crime scene. *Courtesy of Allyson Parrott.*

Laboratory Data Sheet

1. List below the first thing to be done by the first responders at the scene shown in Fig. D.1. What precautions should be taken?

2. What physical evidence should be protected as the first responders arrive at the scene? Circle it in the above figure.

3. What is the process that must be followed by the first responders as they leave the crime scene? Mark it on the scene in Fig. D.1.

DISCUSSION QUESTIONS

1. Is it possible for the first responders to enter a crime scene without changing or altering the crime scene? How should the crime scene investigators handle it?

2. When is the best time for the first responders to prepare a report of their activities? Why?

Exercise E

Multilevel Crime Scene Security

Learning Objectives

- To understand the theory behind and application of multilevel crime scene security to a mock crime scene.
- To use security logs as a means of documenting possible contamination of a crime scene by entry or exit.

All the physical evidence found at the crime scene must remain in its original condition. Its reliability and relevancy is assured when access to the crime scene is restricted or even prevented. The use of a physical barrier is helpful to define the restricted area. Ropes, commercially available crime scene tapes, or signage are commonly used. Official vehicles from the police or fire department can be used successfully in highway, street, or larger outdoor scenes. The barrier's location is significant in that it will locate the area that is to be restricted. The area restricted can be changed dependent on the progress of the crime scene investigation.

A scene security officer should be assigned to intercept anyone trying to enter the general scene area. Restriction to the crime scene should include all nonessential personnel, including police officers or investigators, fire department personnel, witnesses, victim's relatives, neighbors, or bystanders, in addition to members of the news media. A crime scene personnel log should be kept to document *anyone* entering or leaving the crime scene. Limiting traffic through the general area of the crime scene will help to minimize the destruction or loss of physical evidence. Often it is difficult to keep even the most well-intentioned first responders from inadvertently altering the scene. The use of digital photography or even a camera-equipped smartphone to quickly record the crime scene can help to keep the scene secure.

Under ideal circumstances, and with any major case investigation, a *multilevel* approach to crime scene security should be used (see Fig. E.1).

Crime Scene Investigation Laboratory Manual, Second Edition
http://dx.doi.org/10.1016/B978-0-12-812845-9.00005-4

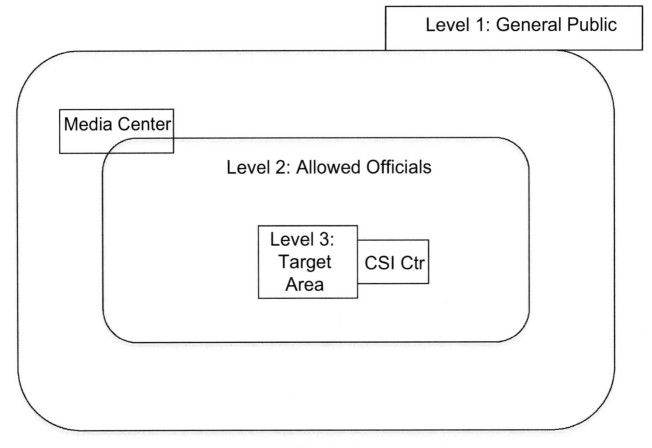

FIGURE E.1   Multilevel crime scene security.

MULTILEVEL CRIME SCENE SECURITY

1. The first level is the outermost perimeter of the general crime scene area, labeled as the overall security level. A scene security officer should be positioned at a designated entry/exit location for this level. It is the job of the security officer at this location to limit the traffic through the scene and to prevent unnecessary personnel from entering. A special area within this first level may be designated for the media; such an area should not be within the next level but should be specifically for the media.
2. The second level of security is set up in an area adjacent to the crime scene. Only police personnel, emergency personnel, support personnel, and any official vehicles such as crime scene vehicles should be allowed in this area. Actions happening within this level will allow for coordination of the crime scene activities, such as briefing the investigators, providing a break and rest area for the scene investigators, and other relevant activities.
3. Level-three security is the crime scene target area. This area should have the strictest control and the highest limit of access. Only the active crime scene investigators should be allowed into this area.

LABORATORY EXERCISE

Laboratory Data Sheet

Given the crime scene shown in Fig. E.2 and using various lines, mark where the crime scene barriers should be placed for correct multilevel crime scene security to be established. The victim's body is located in an interior back bedroom. Also indicate where the security officer should be placed.

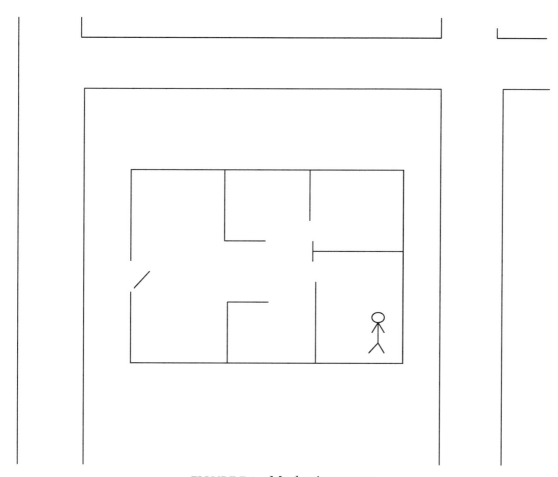

FIGURE E.2   Mock crime scene.

DISCUSSION QUESTIONS

1. What information should be included on the security officer's entry log?

2. When is crime scene security completed? How do you know?

Exercise F

Preliminary Scene Survey

Learning Objectives

- To understand the purpose of a preliminary scene survey and its tasks.
- To practice the application and use of the preliminary survey as part of a mock crime scene investigation.

Once the scene is secure, the crime scene supervisor or the lead crime scene investigator and if available, the case officer should conduct a preliminary crime scene survey or "walk-through." This survey should be done with the first responders, as it is the first responders who have direct knowledge of the original scene appearance and any changes that might have occurred to the scene. The use of digital photography (or even a cellular phone camera) during the survey can be useful for preliminary documentation purposes. The walk-through photographs should not be in great detail; they show an overview of the scene. Because these photographs can be viewed by personnel without actually being in the crime scene, the photos can be used to prevent evidence contamination or loss.

The following is a suggested list of the tasks that should be performed during the crime scene walk-through:

1. Keep in mind that scientific crime scene investigation is objective and systematic. Do not develop "tunnel vision," as it may mislead the direction of the investigation.
2. Note the types of transient and conditional evidence present at the scene. Be aware of weather conditions (and their changeability); light switches on or off; door locks intact or broken; windows opened or closed; heating, ventilation, or air-conditioning status; presence of odors; patterned physical evidence; etc. At this point, documentation, protection, preservation, or collection of these special forms of physical evidence might be necessary.

Crime Scene Investigation Laboratory Manual, Second Edition
http://dx.doi.org/10.1016/B978-0-12-812845-9.00006-6

3. Note the point of entry, point of exit, paths between them, the target area of the scene, types of damage, and any *major* issues or situations (like highway or road closures) involved in the investigation.
4. Attempt to preliminarily answer the following questions: Who? What? Where? When? and How?
5. Access the type of scene: the boundaries, the physical evidence present, and the personnel and equipment needed. In other words, define the crime scene!

LABORATORY EXERCISE

Laboratory Data Sheet

Given the crime scene shown in Fig. F.1, answer the following questions as concisely as possible as they relate to the preliminary scene survey:

FIGURE F.1   Mock crime scene. *Courtesy of Allyson Parrott.*

- *Who?* (Gender of victim(s), approximate age, first responders on scene, others on scene, etc.)

- *What?* (Describe clothes, scene construction, mode of death/injuries, weapons, created/obvious physical evidence, points of entry/exit, etc.)

- *Where?* (Exterior, interior, vehicle, address, etc.)

- *Transient/conditional evidence present?*

DISCUSSION QUESTIONS

1. Write a concise, narrative report based on the information obtained from the preliminary scene survey.

2. Why is (are) the first responder(s) an important part of a preliminary scene survey?

CRIME SCENE DOCUMENTATION

Exercise G

Crime Scene Documentation—Note-Taking

Learning Objectives

- To understand the purpose of notes as a form of record-keeping at the crime scene.
- To apply note-taking to a practical exercise in crime scene documentation.

The first component to document a crime scene is a written record. Generally, the written record of the crime scene investigation must include the investigator's overall observations, actions, and descriptions of the scene and specific identification information such as name, date, telephone number, and address. The legible notes include a *detailed* description of the scene, the victim(s), if applicable, and any items of physical evidence determined to be relevant to the scene. Answering the following questions will assure a complete, detailed description of the scene and evidence: How many (quantity)? What is it (name or other identifier)? Where is it (location)? What does it look like (appearance, color, construction, size, condition, etc.)? Is it unique (serial numbers, signatures, brand or model name, etc.)? Who is at the scene? Who is a potential witness?

The purpose for taking notes as a component of crime scene documentation is to record the scene activities, the location of physical evidence, descriptions of people at the scene, and the condition of the crime scene. Notes are not only crucial for initial crime scene investigation but are also important for any subsequent investigation. Accurate crime scene reporting, valid suspect apprehension, and reliable courtroom testimony are based on the notes and are essential for the successful completion of an investigation and case resolution.

Some basic principles for notes include making the notes permanent, legible, and identifying each page with a sequential page number, the case number, and the note-taker's

Crime Scene Investigation Laboratory Manual, Second Edition
http://dx.doi.org/10.1016/B978-0-12-812845-9.00007-8

name. There is no set process or procedure for crime scene investigation note-taking, but some minimum requirements that should be found in the notes are as follows:

1. Notification and arrival information.
2. Description of the scene.
   (a) Weather (temperature, winds, rain, etc.).
   (b) Location (interior/exterior, first floor/second floor, car/house, etc.).
   (c) Vehicles, buildings, or other major structures.
   (d) Evidence easily identified (prior to preliminary scene survey), especially the transient (smells, sounds, and sights) and conditional (light switches, HVAC controls, etc.) evidence.
3. Description of victim(s)—The victim's body is the single most important piece of evidence in a death investigation. Its condition at the scene is the last time it will be in that condition. It requires significant documentation prior to removal from the scene. Any movement or disruption of the body at the crime scene must be with the authorization or approval of the appropriate authority. Once given, the following may be included in the notes:
   (a) Position or location.
   (b) Lividity or rigidity.
   (c) Wounds.
   (d) Clothing, footwear, jewelry, or forms of identification.
   (e) Weapons at the scene.
   (f) Any physical evidence deposited on the body: patterned evidence, trace evidence, etc.
4. Crime scene investigation team.
   (a) Duty assignments: notes, video, photography, sketching, evidence collection, processing or searching responsibilities, etc.
   (b) Preliminary scene survey information from the walk-through.
   (c) Start and end times for the scene duties.
   (d) Evidence searching, processing or enhancement, collection, packaging, and transportation/storage.

At the conclusion of note-taking as a form of crime scene documentation, the crime scene investigator will need to prepare a report of the crime scene investigation. There is no set format for these reports but certain minimum information must be included to fulfill legal and scientific needs. Fig. G.1 illustrates a suggested format and what to include in the report.

Crime scene report

Documentation within documentation section:
 Writer's name
 Case #
 Scene investigation date
 Report written date
 Scene address
 Time notified, time arrived, time released/cleared
 Page #___ of ___.

Report narrative sections:
 Introduction/team assignments/first responder issues
 Preliminary scene survey
 Scene description
 Body description
 On-scene activities (including but not limited to)
  MEO issues
  Evidence issues:
   Searches
   Enhancement/visualization
   Recovery/packaging/collection
 Subsequent meetings and activities since the on-scene
 activities.

FIGURE G.1   Suggested crime scene report format.

LABORATORY EXERCISE

Laboratory Data Sheet

Given the crime scene shown in Fig. G.2, answer the following questions. Some of the questions may not have an answer as no information is available to the user, but do not leave the space blank. For those situations use "not known at the time of the scene investigation" as the response. You may also be creative in your responses to get practice with your observations.

FIGURE G.2   Mock crime scene 1. *Courtesy of Allyson Parrott.*

1. Describe the scene:
(a) Weather _____

_____

_____

_____

(b) Location_____

_____

_____

_____

(c) Vehicles, buildings, or other major structures _____

_____

_____

_____

(d) Physical evidence _____

_____

_____

_____

2. Description of victim(s):
(a) Position _____

_____

_____

_____

(b) Lividity or rigidity_____

_____

_____

_____

(c) Wounds _____

_____

_____

_____

(d) Clothing, footwear, jewelry, etc._____

_____

_____

_____

(e) Weapons _____

_____

_____

_____

III. CRIME SCENE DOCUMENTATION

(f) Physical evidence deposited on the body_____

_____

_____

_____

3. Crime scene investigation team:

(a) Duty assignment(s) _____

_____

_____

_____

(b) Preliminary scene survey information (walk-through) _____

_____

_____

_____

(c) Start and ending times for the scene duties_____

_____

_____

_____

Repeat the note-taking procedure for the crime scenes shown in Figs. G.3 and G.4.

FIGURE G.3   Mock crime scene 2.

III. CRIME SCENE DOCUMENTATION

FIGURE G.4   Mock crime scene 3.

III. CRIME SCENE DOCUMENTATION

DISCUSSION QUESTIONS

1. Following the suggested format in Fig. G.1, write a narrative, detailed crime scene report for each of the crime scenes in Figs. G.3–G.5. Be sure to include all the details from the notes to fulfill the documentation requirement for each scene (this includes good grammar).

FIGURE G.5   Mock crime scene 4.

2. Should any of the information in your documentation notes be excluded from the scene report? Why or why not?

III. CRIME SCENE DOCUMENTATION

Exercise H

Crime Scene Documentation—Videography

OUTLINE

Learning Objectives

- To learn the purpose of videography as a visual record of the crime scene and its evidence from an orientation viewpoint.
- To learn the proper objective locations for video recording a crime scene.
- To apply videography in practice as a component of crime scene documentation to mock crime scenes.

Video recording of a crime scene is the second component for documentation at the crime scene. "Virtual reality" videography for crime scene documentation as an orientation format has widespread acceptance in the criminal justice community today. The crime scene investigator can use videography as a valuable tool for crime scene documentation, and the use of videography for orientation is essential for any viewer to understand the crime scene and its evidence. Videography at crime scenes should be the first step after the walk-through (or preliminary scene survey) has been completed. It can be done before or just after photography has been done, but before any evidence collection occurs.

The actual process or technique for the videography of crime scenes is summarized below:

1. Start the videography with a placard for documentation. The placard information should include at a minimum the case number, the date, time, and location, the type of crime scene/investigation, and any other *objective* information deemed necessary by the videographer (weather conditions, camera used, etc.).

2. The videography of the entire crime scene should be without any subjective audio recording. In some circumstances, the addition of comments by the videographer may be deemed subjective by the courts and can lead to omissions in the taping process. It is important to prevent added subjectivity to the crime scene documentation by making sure that all law enforcement personnel are not videotaped on the scene. The video should only contain the crime scene, the victim(s), and the physical evidence, not other scene investigators or first responders standing around viewing the process.

3. Begin the orientation of the crime scene videography with a general view of the areas surrounding and leading into or away from the crime scene, such as roads or intersections. A general orientation view of the crime scene should follow the initial recording of the surroundings. The use of the four compass points within the crime scene will ensure that all general viewpoints are taped.

4. Continue videography throughout the crime scene using the wide-angle view format. Close-up views of the items of evidence are not usually part of the videography, as still photography is better suited for that purpose. Videography of the crime scene has the orientation of the crime scene in a graphic nature as its primary purpose and is not intended to allow for detailed, high-quality recording of close-up views of individual items of evidence.

5. The videography of the crime scene should also include a view of the crime scene from the victim's point of view. Standing near the victim's location and recording 360 degrees can achieve this viewpoint and is oftentimes useful for further investigation. However, do not destroy evidence or alter the victim's position when attempting this step.

6. While using videography, use slow camera movements, especially when panning. A tripod or monopod will greatly facilitate these movements. Locating the camera by use of compass points and 360-degree panning will produce recordings with excellent orientation results.

7. Videography of the crime scene, once completed, should never be edited or altered. The original recording should be kept as evidence and duplicate copies made for viewing. There is nothing wrong with repeated recording of the crime scene, especially as new evidence is located or found.

One of the most useful advantages of videography for the crime scene investigator is the ability of the videographer to view and evaluate the recording at the crime scene. Recordings made with digital video cameras in use today can be examined by viewing them through the viewfinder, evaluated immediately, and the entire scene can be rerecorded if necessary. Videography as a documentation technique can provide a perspective of the crime scene that is more easily understood than notes, sketches, or still photographs. Remember, however, that videography is a supplemental technique and not a replacement for the other techniques.

LABORATORY EXERCISE

Respond to the following questions as they relate to Fig. H.1 and H.2.

Laboratory Data Sheet

1. Using a spiral arrow, mark where the crime scene video recordings should occur on the crime scene aerial sketch shown in Fig. H.1. The target crime scene is in the room with the body. No evidence has been found in the structure's other rooms. Hint: There are at least nine spots.
2. Using the placard in Fig. H.2, complete the information that should be included on the beginning placard for your videos in the previous question.
3. Create your own aerial view of a crime scene out in a field. Indicate where the video recordings should be done. Do not forget to create a placard!

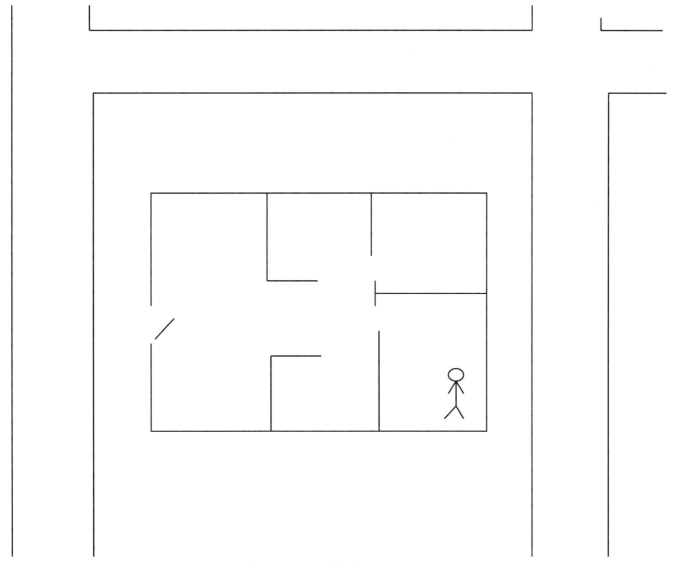

FIGURE H.1 Mock crime scene.

Case No. _____

Date/Time: _____

Name: _____

Description:

FIGURE H.2   Blank video placard.

DISCUSSION QUESTIONS

1. If video recording of a crime scene is not possible at the crime scene, how would the crime scene investigator document the scene? What steps need to be taken?

2. What digital camcorders are available in your area? What are their advantages or disadvantages?

Exercise I

Crime Scene Documentation—Still Photography

Learning Objectives

- To learn proper crime scene documentation using still photography.
- To apply the "two-step approach" to crime scene photography.
- To understand the proper use of shutter speeds, aperture, and focal length for scene photography.
- To understand the concept of depth of field when photographing a crime scene.

The purpose of crime scene photography is to provide a visual record of the scene and related areas, to record a "true and accurate" appearance of the crime scene and physical evidence, to provide investigators and others with the permanent record for subsequent analysis of the scene, and to provide the permanent record to the courts. The traditional method for visual documentation of crime scenes and physical evidence is the use of still photography. Crime scene photography is one of the most important steps in the entire investigation process. Photographing the crime scene is normally done immediately following videography of the scene. If no videography is done, then the still photography of the scene begins immediately following the preliminary scene survey. The systematic, organized method for recording the crime scene and pertinent physical evidence is most often achieved by following a progressive, general-to-specific guideline (see Fig. I.1). This process has been described as going from overall views to mid-range views to close-up views. By following this

FIGURE I.1   Crime scene photography process.

guideline process, the conditions as shown in the photographs give an objective, not subjective representation of the crime scene. The progressive, stepwise nature of the photographs allows for orientation of the crime scene as a whole and the orientation of the evidence within the crime scene. High-quality, high-resolution close-up photography can provide and also provides examination-quality photographs of specific items of evidence. The forensic laboratory for examination purposes may use these photographs when the actual evidence cannot be collected.

The areas surrounding, leading into, or leading out of a crime scene should be photographed at ground level by the scene investigator. Relying upon the use of compass points can facilitate general–overall photographs. For orientation purposes, like videography, overall photographs of the outside of the crime scene should also include views of the exterior of any buildings at which the crime occurred and the windows, doors, pathways/walkways, or other means of entry/exit. Any numerical displays of address or names on the exterior of buildings or structures should be included in an overall photograph of the scene (see Fig. I.2).

FIGURE I.2   Compass points overall photographs.

The documentation of the interior of a crime scene will follow a progressive, stepwise process (see Fig. I.3). An overlapping technique of photographs may assist with the total documentation of the area. As the photographer enters completely inside the interior crime scene, using the four compass points or corners will assist with achieving total recording of the scene. These photographs will depict the overall view of the scene and, as the mid-range photographs are taken, will focus on the items of evidence found in the scene. Any connecting rooms or adjacent areas need to be included in the overall orientation photographs.

Interior overlapping photographs: The individual items of physical evidence need to be photographed with a mid-range photograph for orientation purposes, followed by a close-up or examination-quality photograph. The mid-range photograph will show how the item of evidence is related to its surroundings, and the close-up photograph will document individualizing details of the item (see Fig. I.4). A number or other marker may identify individual items of evidence.

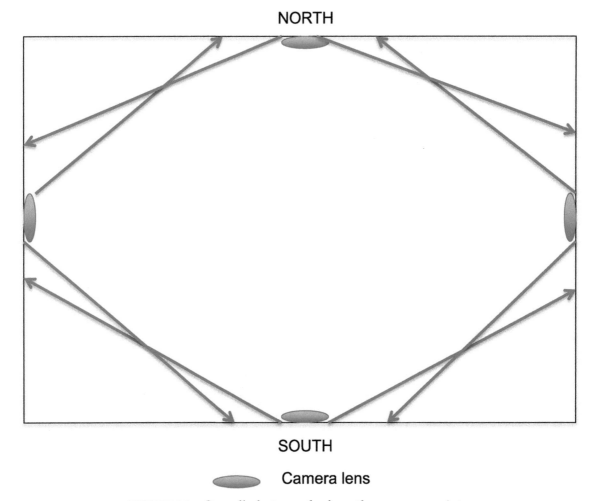

NORTH

SOUTH

Camera lens

FIGURE I.3   Overall photographs from the compass points.

Overall to specific photographs: All of the photographs taken as part of crime scene documentation must be chronologically recorded. The common procedure used for this purpose is the maintenance of the *photo log*. The log is the complete written record of all the photographic documentation at the crime scene. The log should include the name of the photographer, case number, date/location of the incident, and documentation. Every photograph taken as part of the crime scene investigation must be recorded in the log. Variables of the photographs that must be recorded are as follows:

1. Date and time of exposure
2. Roll number and exposure number or image card number with image number
3. Type of photograph taken (overall, mid-range, or close up)
4. Distance between camera and subject for close-up photos
5. Camera settings (lens focal length, f/stop, and shutter speed)
6. Use of tripod or flash (with setting)
7. Brief description of photograph

FIGURE I.4   Overall to specific photographs.

The log must also include the photography equipment documentation:

1. Make, model, and type of camera
2. Camera serial number
3. Lens make, model (focal length), and serial number
4. Flash information (make, model, and serial number)

While most digital cameras have the ability to take very good photographs at most crime scenes, the crime scene investigator must be able to manually adjust the photographic exposure. The scene photographer must constantly monitor the images for correct exposure. The correct exposure of a crime scene photograph is dependent on the amount of light traveling through the lens on the camera. Besides the use of an electronic flash attachment, the correct exposure can be obtained with proper aperture and shutter speed use. Fig. I.5 shows various aperture (f/stop) and shutter speed effects. Crime scene photography must balance aperture and shutter speed to get good scene photographs.

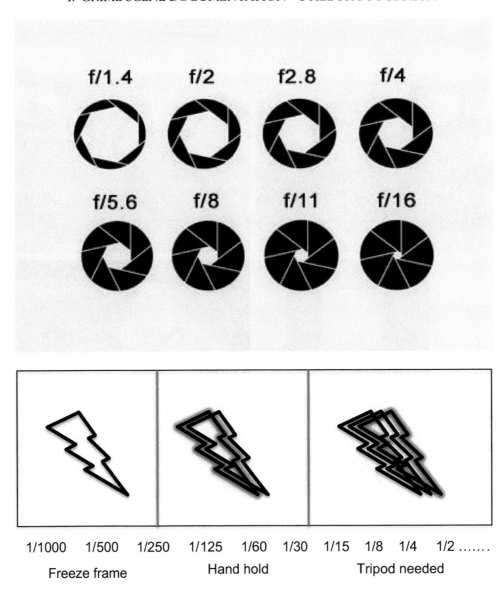

FIGURE I.5   Aperture openings and shutter speeds.

LABORATORY EXERCISE

The following exercise will allow for practice by the photographer to learn the proper locations to photographically document a crime scene, prepare a proper photo log, practice the "two-step" approach for documenting a crime scene from overall views to close-up photographs of evidence, and understand the relationship of aperture and shutter speed as applied to depth of field situations.

Laboratory Data Sheet

Part One: Compass Point Overall Photographs

Using Fig. I.6, mark with an arrow to show the direction of the photograph that would be taken to document the exterior overall views of this crime scene.

Part Two: Photo Log and Introductory Placard

Set up a mock interior crime scene with at least two items of evidence. Prepare a photo log template for the crime scene photographs that will be taken to document this

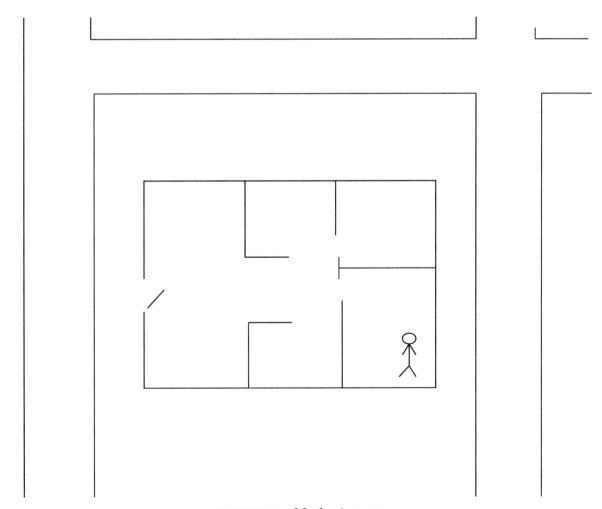

FIGURE I.6   Mock crime scene.

scene. Use a case number, date, and description appropriate for the log. Do not forget the headings on the log (image number, time, description, shutter speed, aperture, focal length, etc.).

Part Three: Progressive Photographs of the Crime Scene and Evidence

Using your mock crime scene from Part Two, skip the necessary exterior overall photographs and move to the photography of the interior of your scene. Using a digital camera, take the overlapping overall photographs of the target area, followed by the mid-range and close-up photographs of items of evidence. You may need to make your own evidence markers. Be sure to fill the frame of the close-up photographs.

Part Four: Balancing Aperture and Shutter Speeds—Depth of Field
Aperture Priority Exercise

Place a paper clip, a short pencil, a ballpoint pen, and a six-inch ruler in a drinking glass. Mount your camera on a tripod and set the camera to A or aperture priority (this setting will allow the camera to automatically adjust the shutter speed based on your aperture setting). Starting with the widest aperture (f/2.8), take an "in-focus" photograph of the glass and contents from a top view to downward. Repeat for the apertures shown in Chart I.1. Complete the chart using the suggested apertures.

CHART I.1   Aperture Priority and Depth of Fielf

Aperture	Shutter Speed (Set by Camera)	Number of Items in Focus in Glass	Photo Assessment (Blurry, Dark, etc)
f/2.8			
f/4			
f/5.6			
f/8			
f/11			
f/16			
f/22			

Conclusion: What generally happened to the depth of field, the amount of objects in focus from the tip of the pencil to the paper clip, as the f/stop number got larger (or the aperture opening got smaller)?

Shutter Speed Priority Exercise

Using the same objects described in the previous activity and with the camera still mounted on a tripod for an above view, set the camera with a shutter speed priority or S setting (the camera will automatically set the appropriate aperture). Following Chart I.2, photograph the drinking glass.

Conclusion: What generally happened to the quality of the photographs as the shutter speed increased?

CHART I.2   Shutter Speed Priority and Depth of Field

Shutter Speed (sec)	Aperture (Set by Camera)	Number of Items in Focus in Glass	Photo Assessment (Blurry, Dark, etc)
1/2			
1/10			
1/30			
1/60			
1/125			
1/250			
1/1000			

DISCUSSION QUESTIONS

1. What needs to be added to a close-up photograph if patterned evidence is present? How will that be accomplished?

2. What special equipment can be used to facilitate the overall documentation of a crime scene?

3. What two factors are being balanced to get good exposure and "in-focus" photographs at a crime scene? Which activities illustrated this balance?

SPECIAL TOPIC LASER SCANNERS AT CRIME SCENES

Three-dimensional scanners using lasers have found their way to crime scenes. Laser scanning, a visual image form of documentation of crime scenes, has been coupled with accurate measurement capabilities. Various types of lasers are commonly used for survey and measurements at scenes, but software programs allow for 3-D images to be recorded and viewpoints to be changed. Furthermore, 3-D images can be used to present to investigators and juries "virtual, fly-through" views of the crime scene and physical evidence (see Fig. I.7). Continued improvement and evolution of these scanners has greatly increased their accepted use. Cost-effective, hand-held, or tripod-mounted scanners are more and more commonly used to document scenes and evidence.

FIGURE I.7   Three-dimensional laser scanner sitemap of a mock crime scene.

Exercise J

Crime Scene Documentation—Sketching

Learning Objectives

- To learn proper sketching as a form of crime scene documentation.
- To identify various measurement techniques for use at the crime scene.
- To identify various forms of crime scene sketches.
- To apply the different measurement techniques and types of sketches to mock crime scenes.

The final component of crime scene documentation is the preparation of the crime scene sketch or diagram. Sketching at the crime scene is not about drawing; it is about *measuring*. Sketching is quantitative. Still photography is a two-dimensional representation of three-dimensional areas and items. It will, therefore, inherently result in some distortion of the spatial relationship of objects in the photographs. Common examples of the distortions are found in the reconstruction of shooting trajectories or bloodshed points of origin.

The crime scene sketch is the permanent record of the actual size and distance relationships between the crime scene and its physical evidence. The sketch must correlate and supplement the still photographs taken at the scene. The sketch further supports the relevancy, reliability, and validity of physical evidence found at the crime scene.

Crime scene sketch preparation requires some planning and organizational skills by the crime scene investigator. There are two basic types of crime scene sketches that are part of a crime scene investigation: a *rough sketch* and a *to-scale, finished,* or *final sketch* (see Fig. J.1). There are two basic types of perspectives that are used for crime scene sketches: the *overhead* or "bird's-eye view" and the *elevation* or "side view" (see Fig. J.2). There are other variations to these two types of sketches but they are the most common.

A *rough sketch* is made at the crime scene before evidence collection. It shows all the evidence to be collected, major structures present in the crime scene, and other

Rough Sketch: *(Courtesy of Ashley Dumbrill)*

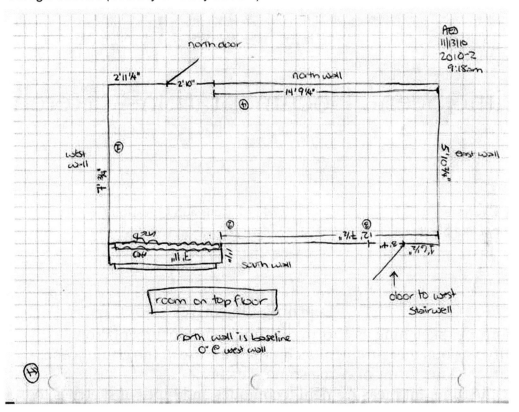

Final Sketch:

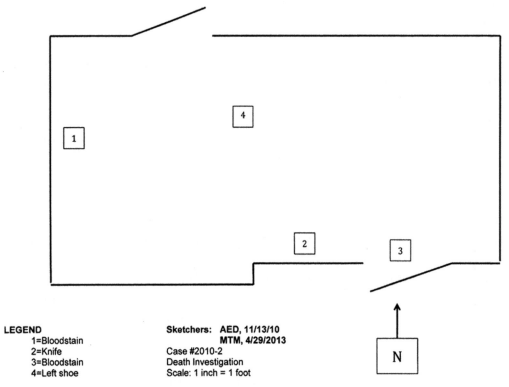

FIGURE J.1   Rough and final sketches.

III. CRIME SCENE DOCUMENTATION

Overhead Sketch:

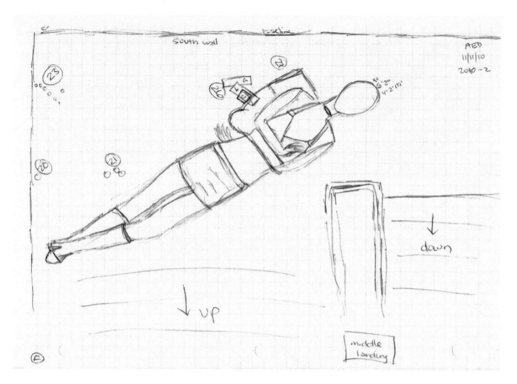

Projected View Sketch

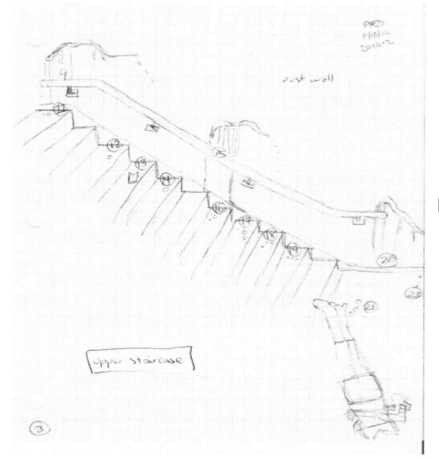

FIGURE J.2 Overhead sketch and projected view sketch.

III. CRIME SCENE DOCUMENTATION

FIGURE J.3   Three-dimensional sketch.

relevant structures in or near the crime scene. The rough sketch will show all the measurements taken to determine the size and distance relationships at the crime scene. A *final* or *finished sketch*, drawn to scale, is prepared from the rough sketch. The final sketch is normally prepared for courtroom presentation and reconstruction purposes. It will show the relevant structures within the crime scene and all items of evidence. It should never show any measurements. It has a clean, uncluttered appearance for ease of viewing and use.

A crime scene sketch is usually drawn from a looking-down or *overhead* perspective. This type of perspective is the most common type and is most recognizable by other investigators and juries. The *side-view* sketch can be used for supplementing the still photography documentation. The crime scene sketcher should be prepared to combine sketch types and add photographs to supplement the documentation. Digital drawing programs along with digital images make this an easily accomplished task. Three-dimensional sketching is not normally done, but measurements can be used in a number of computer-aided drawing programs and can occasionally be used for 3-D model construction (see Fig. J.3).

There are three commonly used measuring techniques for sketching the crime scene and evidence: *triangulation, polar coordinates*, and *base line* or *fixed line*. All three measurement techniques (see Fig. J.4) are based upon the determination of fixed, or known, starting points. The fixed points should be permanent; however, the name "fixed" indicates a known location, not necessarily permanency.

Triangulation:

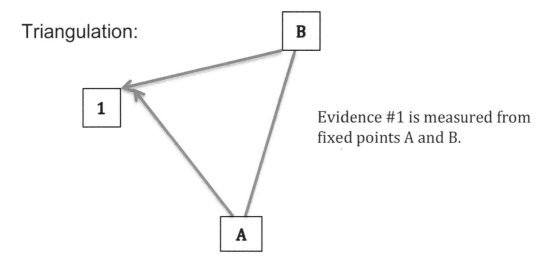

Evidence #1 is measured from fixed points A and B.

Polar coordinates:

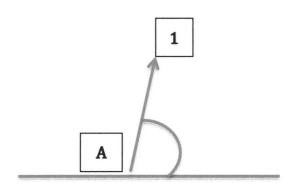

Evidence #1 is measured from fixed point A and the angle of incident.

Base line:

Base-line location is fixed.

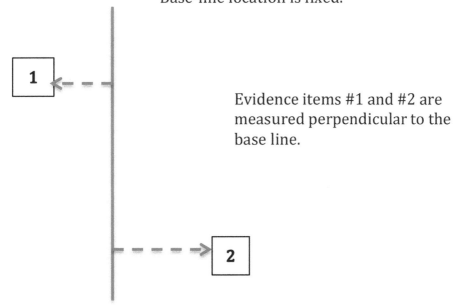

Evidence items #1 and #2 are measured perpendicular to the base line.

FIGURE J.4 Crime scene measurement techniques.

III. CRIME SCENE DOCUMENTATION

1. *Triangulation*—Select two fixed points, measure the distance between them, and prepare a basic layout sketch of the scene with the points included. Every item of evidence is then measured from these two points.
2. *Polar coordinates*—From a fixed point, all evidence is measured for distance from the point and is measured for direction or angle. The angle is measured by the use of a protractor or other survey instruments (laser transit equipment is frequently used).
3. *Base line or fixed line*—Establish a straight line or base line between two fixed points. The items of evidence will be measured along the fixed line and at perpendiculars to the line. A variation of this technique, rectangulation, uses two perpendicular lines (three fixed points). The evidence is measured from these perpendicular lines.

The crime scene sketch must include not only the measurements of the crime scene and the physical evidence but also other important documentation information. The information to be included in this portion of the sketch is as follows:

1. Agency case number
2. Offense or incident type (death investigation, burglary, etc.)
3. Victim(s) name(s): never place a suspect's name on the sketch
4. Address or location
5. Scene describer (interior of house, outdoor area of scene, room 222, etc.) including weather and lighting conditions
6. Date and time the sketch was started
7. Sketcher's name, assistant sketcher's name, or verifier's name
8. Scale used (for example, 1 mm = 1 inch)
9. Legend (# = item of evidence) of physical evidence

A tool added to the sketching documentation function at the crime scene is a laser-scanning measuring and sketching system. This tool uses laser scanners with software programs to replace bulky or cumbersome tapes and sketch pads. The system will generate to-scale images at the crime scene and allow for integration with videography and sketching. Fig. J.5 shows a scanning-laser-generated 3-D sketch. Some laser-scanning programs of crime scenes allow for some pseudoanimation with imbedded photographs too.

An additional form of crime scene sketching documentation is the use of to-scale crime scene models. The use of scale models necessitates the taking of many detailed measurements, is time consuming, and requires the use of photographs, drawings, and, often, structural blueprints. Scale models are very useful for presenting reconstructions to juries. Computer animations have gained some popularity in crime scene investigations and can be aided by the use of the digital documentation in general.

FIGURE J.5 Laser-scanner sketch of crime scene.

LABORATORY EXERCISE

Laboratory Data Sheet

Set up your own mock crime scene in a medium-sized room. Put at least five pieces of evidence in your scene. Use case number 012,345, and consider yourself to be dispatched by an agency of your choice. You are the team's crime scene sketcher. Using the graph paper forms provided, measure and create a rough sketch of your scene using the following parameters:

1. Use an overhead view, and measure using the triangulation measurement technique.
2. Use an overhead view, and measure using the base-line measurement technique.
3. Use one or both of the rough sketches you created in steps 1 or 2 to prepare a finished sketch on a separate sheet of paper. Remember it is drawn to scale with measurements shown. Do not forget the documentation information!

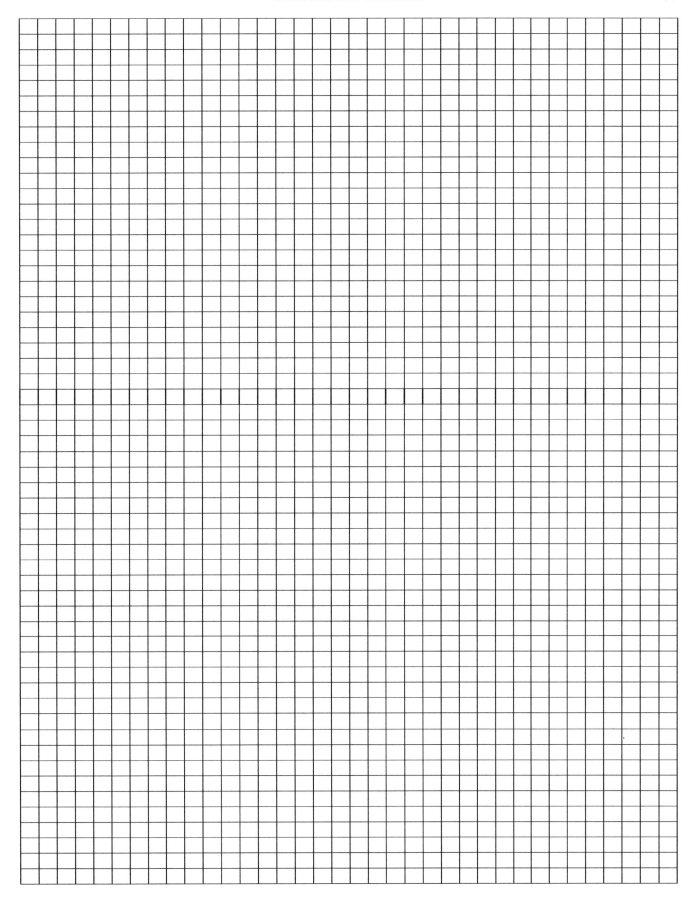

III. CRIME SCENE DOCUMENTATION

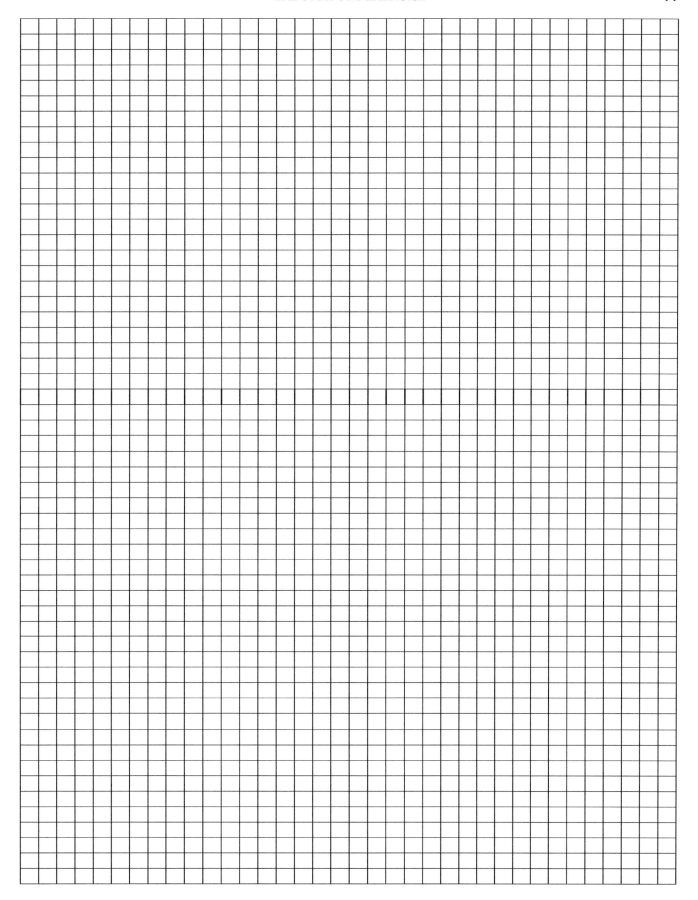

III. CRIME SCENE DOCUMENTATION

DISCUSSION QUESTIONS

1. For all of the sketches you made, what was included in them?

2. If a footwear impression in blood was present in your scene, would you sketch it along with photographic documentation? Why or why not?

3. Which method of measurement worked the best for your interior crime scene? Would you use it for a large outdoor crime scene? Why or why not?

PHYSICAL EVIDENCE AT CRIME SCENES

Exercise K

Physical Searches

Learning Objectives

- To understand the scientific principles for intensively searching the crime scene.
- To identify the areas of highest probability for finding evidence at the scene.
- To identify the geometric search patterns commonly used to intensively search at crime scenes.
- To apply the searching techniques to a mock crime scene scenario.

Physical evidence obtained from the crime scene contributes greatly to the successful outcome of the case investigation. Although it is theoretically possible that a perfect crime has been committed with the perpetrator leaving minimal physical evidence, it is more likely that the critical evidence was *never found*. The other tasks performed at a crime scene can be learned, but the simple task of finding that critical evidence *must never be* the failed task of the crime scene investigation. The successful search for evidence will only occur when crime scene investigators understand the objectiveness of a crime scene search and rely on a systematic, structured, science-based search process.

OBJECTIVES OF A CRIME SCENE SEARCH

The goal of a crime scene search is to locate all potentially relevant and meaningful physical evidence that could be used to link or exonerate a suspect, victim, or witness to a crime. A seasoned crime scene investigator will possess good instincts as to where the relevant evidence will likely be located. Like the scientific method a good crime scene search is a systematic and structured basic approach. Underlying the search process are two general issues: Where should you look for the evidence and how should you actually conduct the search process?

GENERAL CONCEPTS OF CRIME SCENE SEARCHES

Although the preliminary scene survey provides the investigators with some idea as to evidence at the crime scene, to search a crime scene properly for physical evidence it is necessary to view the crime scene in its entirety and not just from the perspective of evidence collection. To accomplish this task, it is useful to examine areas that you normally do not examine. Also, look for evidence from different vantage points, for example, at floor level and at an elevated level. It is extremely important to be cautious and take the time necessary for a methodical, systematic search. This approach ensures that critical evidence will not be damaged or overlooked. Also, look for what is not present or what is missing from the scene. The skillful, experienced crime scene investigator develops a "logic of the scene" to facilitate the search.

FIGURE K.1 Disappearing bloody footwear impressions *do not* mean that the source is flying away. *Courtesy of Allison Parrott.*

Although there are numerous exceptions, specific crimes regularly generate different kinds of physical evidence. Excellent and productive crime scene searches are based on logic and an analytical approach to the particular scene. Although there is an inherent danger of jumping to conclusions and losing objectivity, it is most beneficial to logically deduce the types of evidence expected and potential locations of that evidence based on the general type of crime committed (see Fig. K.1). For every crime scene there are areas at the scene that have the highest probability of containing evidence. These, for areas, are the point of entry, the point of exit, the path between the points of entry/exit, and the focal point in the crime scene, such as the body or the counter at a store that has been robbed.

CRIME SCENE SEARCH PATTERNS

Crime scene search patterns are varied, are outwardly different in style and application, and provide a structure and organization to ensure that no physical evidence is missed at the crime scene. There is no single correct search method for a specific type of crime scene. Most of the basic search patterns employ a geometric pattern (see Fig. K.2). The six basic search patterns are the line, grid, spiral, ray, zone, and link methods. If there is any doubt that some evidence may have been overlooked, then an easy-to-use, basic search method should be employed. Note that some search methods are better suited for outdoor scenes, whereas others work best for indoor crime scenes. Of course, any physical evidence found must be immediately documented using the techniques discussed in earlier exercises.

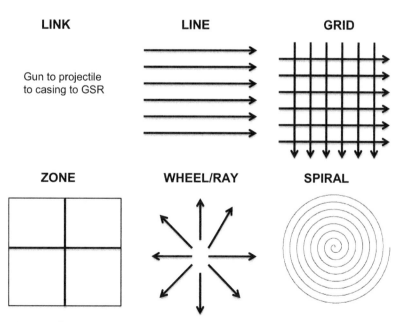

FIGURE K.2 Six geometric search patterns.

Link Method

The link method is a productive and common approach for crime scene searches. This method is based on the four-way linkage theory, seeking to find associations between the scene, victim, suspect, and physical evidence. It is a systematic and logical method of gathering physical evidence that can be linked to a particular crime or activity. Although this method is not a geometric pattern or easily definable, it is nonetheless a systematic approach. For example, a victim with a gunshot wound leads to a firearm, a projectile, casings, gunshot residue, etc. The linkages are applications of common logic.

Line (STRIP) Method

Outdoor crime scenes can be large in scope and difficult to search because of vegetation, topography, water, and area to cover. One of the easiest patterns to employ that is still very effective is the line method. This geometric pattern involves the establishing of a series of lines or strips in the scene. Members of the search team are arranged at regular intervals, usually arm's length and proceed to search along straight lines. The investigator identifies any evidence in the path. This method is well suited for searching large areas, such as parks, fields, yards, parking lots, or highways. The members of the search team are not necessarily trained crime scene investigators, but they are given explicit instructions as to how to search and what they are looking for, and they are instructed to stop, do not touch, and immediately notify one of the crime scene investigators if they find anything suspicious or valuable.

Grid Method

The grid method is a modified double-line search. In this approach, a line pattern is constructed then a second line pattern is established in the same area, running perpendicular to the first line pattern. On completing the first line pattern, the searchers realign on the other line pattern. Thus, the same area is searched twice by a grid pattern format. An additional advantage is that two different searchers search the same area. Although this method is more time consuming, it is more thorough and methodical.

Zone Method

Crime scenes that have definable zones can be searched by focusing on the zones in a systematic manner. Indoor crime scenes are examples of such a scene. Depending on the size of the scene, each zone may be subdivided as needed until it is of manageable size. Critical zones such as target areas, point of entry, and point of exit can be searched multiple times.

Wheel/Ray Method

With the wheel method, the investigators start from a critical point and travel outward along many straight lines, or rays, from this point. This search pattern becomes increasingly difficult when searching larger areas and is therefore usually used only for special scene situations and in limited applications. This method can also be used on a smaller scale. Suppose the "scene" consists of the victim's body or clothing; a detailed search may be conducted by starting at a central point and proceeding outward in all directions.

Spiral Method

Similar to the wheel/ray method, the spiral method considers the crime scene large and circular in design. There are two techniques commonly used for spiral methods; one method is generally referred to as an inward spiral, and the other is an outward spiral. In addition, the search can be in either a clockwise or counterclockwise direction. It may be beneficial to conduct the search twice, in opposite directions. This method is commonly used by the military and must be aided by the use of navigational tools.

LABORATORY EXERCISE

For this exercise the user will respond to the questions that relate to a mock crime scene shown in Fig. K.3.

Laboratory Data Sheet

1. Using the crime scene shown in Fig. K.3, identify the type of geometric search pattern you would use and then mark the search paths on the scene.

2. With the same scene in mind, identify a second physical search pattern that could be used for the scene.

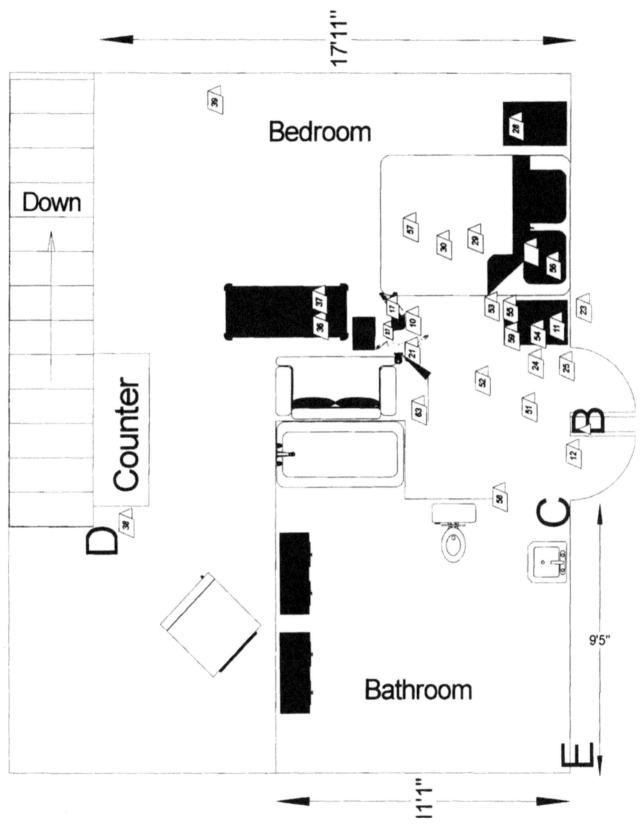

FIGURE K.3   Mock crime scene.

IV. PHYSICAL EVIDENCE AT CRIME SCENES

DISCUSSION QUESTIONS

1. Could a crime scene be searched using all of the geometric patterns discussed? If so, what types of scenes? Sketch an example.

2. What should the searchers be doing while they are "on their pattern searches"? What should they not do?

Exercise L

Visualization and Enhancement: Lighting Aids

Exercises covering how to utilize UV lights and other commonly obtained Alternate Light Sources (ALSs).

Learning Objectives

- To identify various types of lighting aids for searching and visualizing evidence at the crime scene.
- To identify alternate light sources (ALSs) that are used to search for a variety of evidence.
- To identify various types of evidence, select ALS and select the barrier filter for the evidence.
- To apply the knowledge of lighting aids at a mock crime scene scenario.

It seems obvious that any search will be helped by the use of lighting aids. A simple flashlight held at a low angle should be used for the geometric search patterns from the last exercise (see Exercise K). However, a search for physical evidence using only visible wavelengths of light may not always reveal all the evidence present. Depending on the composition or type of the surface on which the physical evidence has been deposited, wavelengths of light beyond the visible spectrum are useful. The fluorescence, absorbance, reflectance, and luminescence of physical evidence when exposed to these various wavelengths with viewing-barrier filters is used for evidence enhancement and therefore for locating the evidence. Portable ALSs with varying wavelengths and power capabilities are common and must be used to assure a good search.

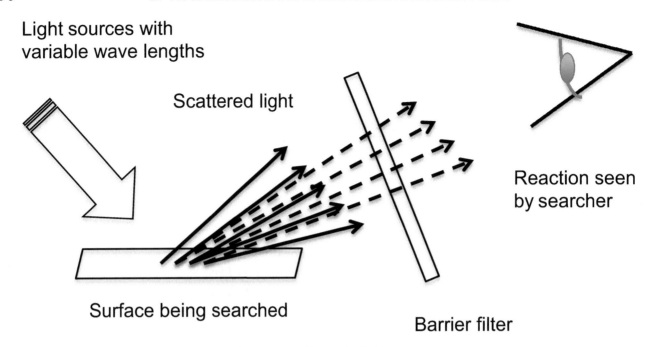

FIGURE L.1   Alternate light sources.

In general, an ALS is a light source with a filtering system to allow specific wavelengths of light from ultraviolet to infrared wavelengths to be emitted (or screened out). Accessories such as colored screens or barrier filters can be used, allowing for the fluorescence of the light to be seen (see Fig. L.1).

SPECIFIC EVIDENCE APPLICATIONS

Latent Fingerprint Detection

This remains the primary evidence type benefitting from the use of an ALS. Fluorescent enhancement techniques are greatly complemented by the use of an ALS (see Exercise O). ALS fingerprint detection also works on highly textured, fluorescent, fragile, and contaminated surfaces. The most common ALS wavelengths used for the detection of latent fingerprints are 445–455 nm (blue light) with an orange barrier filter. See Fig. L.2.

Body Fluids

Most body fluids, including semen, saliva, and vaginal fluids, are basically fluorescent. Therefore, the use of an ALS is essential for visualization and enhancement. Ultraviolet (UV) lights have a long history of assisting in the search for body fluids, but many of the surfaces on which the fluids are deposited will also fluoresce with UV light. For this reason, an ALS with longer wavelengths (540 nm or green) will eliminate the substrate background interference. Barrier filters of orange and yellow are needed. ALSs with more power and offering more wavelength options are best for the enhancement of a variety of body fluids.

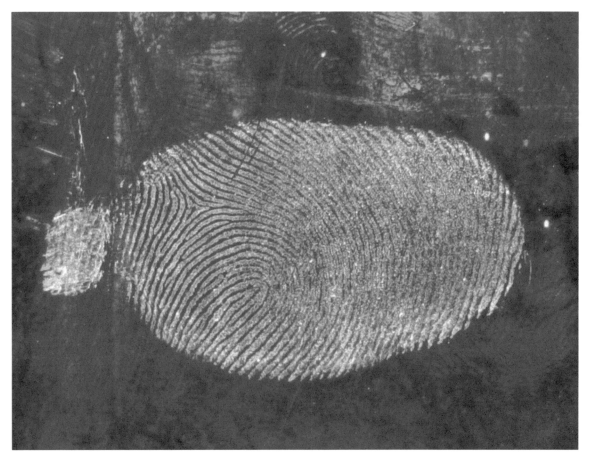

FIGURE L.2   Fingerprint found by Alternate light source.

Hairs and Fibers

The use of side lighting with conventional white light such as a flashlight is the best way to search for hairs and fibers at crime scenes. No barrier filters are necessary for white light ALS searching. If background interference is encountered, then the use of blue wavelength ALS with orange barrier filters can be used to visualize this trace evidence. Chemically treated hair can be found with other wavelengths and corresponding filters.

Bruises/Bite Marks/Pattern Wounds

Bruise patterns can exist in a variety of colors or in such small amounts that they may not always be seen using conventional white light. With these difficult patterns, an ALS with the capability of offering a variety of wavelengths is necessary.

Other Evidence Types

ALSs have a variety of applications for a variety of other evidence types not discussed previously (see Table L.1). These other types of evidence include questioned documents, GSR, explosive residues, bone fragments, footwear patterns, drugs, etc. A portable, powerful ALS with a variety of wavelength options is an excellent crime scene search instrument.

TABLE L.1   Alternate Light Source Wavelengths for Evidence Types

Evidence Type	Wavelength (nm)	Barrier Filter
Bodily fluids, semen	395 (UV), 455	None, orange, yellow
Bone fragments	395 (UV), 455	Orange, yellow
Blood stains (untreated)	395 (UV)	None
Latents in oils, grease	455	Orange
TRACE EVIDENCE ON		
Blue/green bkds	595	Orange, yellow
Trace evidence generally	625	None, yellow

PHOTOGRAPHIC METHODS

The photography of ALS enhancements must be performed like that of all other evidence. Most cameras have the capability of adjusting the exposure for the ALS fluorescence, reflectance, absorbance, or luminescence given off by the evidence type. The difficulty is that the image must be photographed using the barrier filter placed in front of the lens and that may further reduce the quantity of light entering the camera (See Fig. L.3).

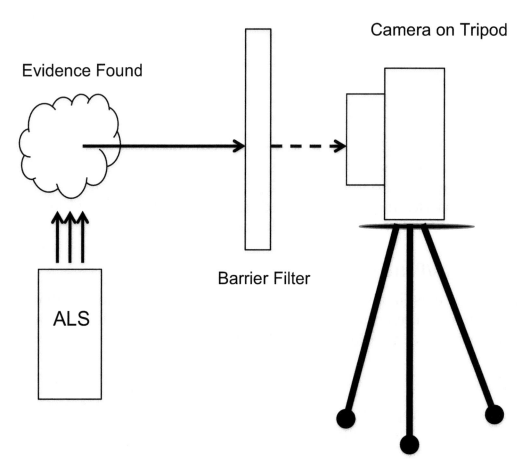

FIGURE L.3   Photograph with Alternate light source.

LABORATORY EXERCISES

For this exercise, two scenarios will be used with two different ALSs. Any visualized evidence will be documented with photography.

Laboratory Data Sheet

Part A. White Light and Side Lighting

1. Retrieve a blanket from home or another source. Using a white light ALS (flashlight) and holding the light at a side angle, locate any trace evidence such as hairs and fibers. Draw a sketch of the blanket with the fibers/hairs located.

2. Using the same technique, search the floor space of a mock crime scene of your choice. Once any trace evidence has been found, photograph the evidence appropriately and assign it individual evidence numbers.

Part B. Handheld Alternate Light Source (If Available)

1. Use the same blanket from Part A. Use an ALS that is set at 445–455 nm or a blue-light setting with an orange barrier filter. This time, search for trace evidence. Document with a sketch the evidence found.
2. Set up a new mock crime scene. Be sure to plant fingerprints on a shiny surface and some other physiological fluid on another surface. Search with a geometric pattern using a blue light with an orange filter. Document with notes and photography.
3. A second search of the scene in step 2 should now be done with an ALS with longer wavelengths (540 nm or green) and a clear or yellow barrier filter. Photograph any found, evidence and identify its category as fingerprint, trace evidence, or physiological fluid.

DISCUSSION QUESTIONS

1. Do ALSs have any applications in a laboratory setting? How would you use one?

2. What new application for using an ALS would facilitate a search for evidence in a criminal investigation you have seen on television?

3. Will ALS devices require complete darkness at the crime scene to be properly used?

Exercise M

Visualization and Enhancement: Biological Evidence

Learning Objectives

- To understand and apply the use of heme-based color reagents for pattern enhancement and preliminary identification screening purposes of biological evidence.
- To understand and apply the use of protein dye-staining reagents for pattern enhancement and preliminary identification screening purposes of biological evidence.

Enhancement reagents and field tests, also called preliminary screening tests, provide valuable assistance in crime scene searching and the locating of biological physical evidence not readily seen as part of the preliminary scene survey. These reagents and tests are also designed for pattern enhancement (reconstruction possibilities), screening evidence at the crime scene, and giving detectives immediate information about possible evidence to assist with an investigation.

Generally, these field tests are widely used and are capable of detecting biological materials or chemical substances (see Exercise N). To be effective and useful in field applications, these reagents and tests should be relatively easy to use at the crime scene, require little specialized equipment, be as sensitive and specific as possible, be timely, be easy to interpret, and utilize only small amounts of a sample during testing.

Enhancement reagents are used to visualize and to increase the color contrast of transfer pattern evidence such as bloodstains, fingerprints, footprints, shoe imprints, and other physical patterns. Also, in some instances, enhancement reagents have dual purposes: presumptive tests for biological substances and the enhancement of physical patterns.

BIOLOGICAL EVIDENCE ENHANCEMENT REAGENTS

Blood enhancement reagents (and field tests) fall into two basic groups depending on the chemical reactivity of the evidence and the reagent chosen: hemoglobin (heme group) or protein-reacting reagents.

Hemoglobin (Heme)-Based Enhancement Reagents

These enhancement reagents are designed to detect minute traces of heme or heme-like derivatives. The hemoglobin molecule with its iron-rich heme in the red blood cells is responsible for carrying oxygen through the body. The iron heme is easily oxidized (to carry the oxygen). The enhancement reagents are based on that oxidation reactivity and undergo a classic oxidation–reduction reaction. The reaction will convert a reduced-form, colorless reagent to a colored by-product, now oxidized, that can seen by the crime scene searcher (see Fig. M.1 and Chart M.1).

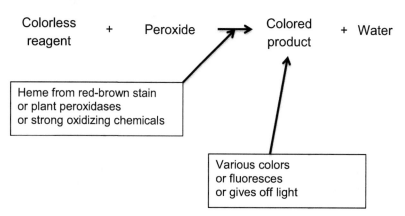

FIGURE M.1   Chemical basis for heme-based reagents.

Reagent	Result
Phenolphthalein (Kastle-Mayer)	Pink/red/violet
Ortho-Tolidine (o-Tol)	Blue/violet
Tetramethylbenzidine (TMB)	Blue/green
Leucocrystal violet (LCV)	Blue/violet
Fluorescein	ALS fluorescence with filter
Luminol	Photo luminescent (blue-white light)

CHART M.1   Heme-based enhancement reagents.

The most commonly used heme-based reagents are phenolphthalein (Kastle–Meyer (KM)), orthotolidine, tetramethylbenzidine (TMB), leucocrystal violet (LCV), fluorescein, and luminol. Fluorescein has a positive result in the form of a product that fluoresces but must be visualized using an alternate light source (ALS). With luminol, a positive test is indicated by photoluminescence rather than a visual color formation. A positive reaction, as indicated by the formation of a colored, fluorescent, or illuminating product, merely indicates the possibility of the presence of blood (see Fig. M.2). There are many substances that will also catalyze this same reaction such as plant peroxidase or strong chemical oxidants. It is essential for the crime scene investigator to make sure that the testing reagents have been tested on known standards of blood prior to testing the suspected stains; the lack of a reaction on the unknown stain can be deemed to mean that blood is absent.

The application of these enhancement reagents is generally done by a sequential spraying process directly on the surfaces at the crime scene. Any colored products are immediately documented using appropriate methods. Because the colored products can fade or change over a short period of time, the documentation processes are easily done with preparation prior to spraying. Additional spraying can be done, but overspraying can wash away patterns and samples for collection. *Be careful not to overspray!*

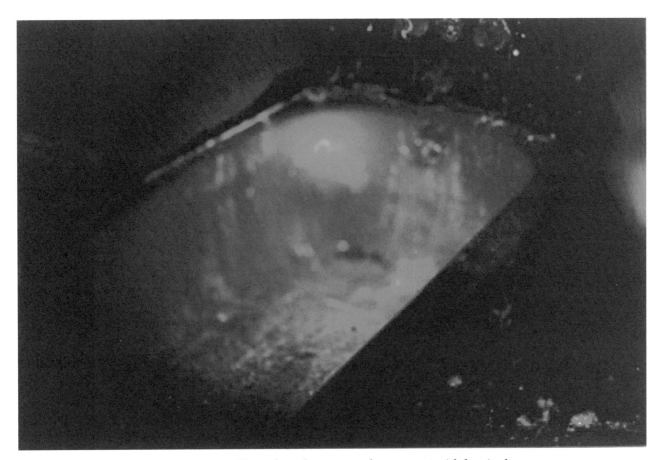

FIGURE M.2 Heme-based pattern enhancement with luminol.

IV. PHYSICAL EVIDENCE AT CRIME SCENES

Field tests are usually a sequential system of reagent drops added to the swabbed samples of the unknown scene evidence. Positive results are immediate with color changes easily observed. The laboratory exercise ahead will illustrate this procedure.

Protein-Reacting-Based Enhancement Reagents

There are a variety of biological protein-containing materials present at a crime scene. Proteins are composed of chemical units called amino acids. The detection of protein-containing evidence is based on the reactivity of the amino acids. Proteins are components in many body tissues and fluids, including skin, tissue, blood, and milk. A suspect or victim may deposit large or trace quantities of these substances at a crime scene, even during relatively minor contact. Common sources of protein located at a crime scene are associated with contact transfer or a direct deposit of body fluids, such as sweat, tears, blood, urine, semen, or saliva. Protein residues from latent fingerprints, palm prints, footprints, lip prints, and ear prints can be located by the use of amino-acid-detecting reagents such as ninhydrin, Amido Black, and, if blood is suspected, bloody-print-enhancement reagents. Each of these reagents has slightly different sensitivities, limitations, and methods of application (immersion or spraying); however, they all are proven to be very effective at locating and/or enhancing evidence containing proteins (amino acids). Many of the recently developed protein-staining reagents require the use of ALSs to assist visualization. These enhancement reagents will be discussed in Exercise O. See Fig. M.3 for a list of the protein-based reagents.

Reagent	Result	Application	Miscellaneous
Ninhydrin	Purple stains	Spraying or immersion	Works best on older stains
Amido black	Black dye staining	Spraying or immersion	Difficult with dark backgrounds
Coomassie blue	Violet dye staining	Spraying	Requires a clarifying solution
Crowle's double stain	Dye staining	Spraying	Not an organic solution
1,8-Diazafluoren-9-one (DFO)	Dye staining	Spraying	After ninhydrin, 495-550 nm, red
Ardox	Fluorescent	Spraying or immersion	ALS 435-480 nm, yellow filter
Rhodamine 6G	Fluorescent	Spraying or immersion	ALS 495-550 nm, red filter

FIGURE M.3   Protein-staining enhancement reagents.

FIELD TESTS FOR BIOLOGICAL EVIDENCE

Suspected Blood Evidence

The field tests for blood are primarily based on the same oxidation–reduction reaction used above for enhancement while searching (see Chart M.1). The general procedure is a dropwise addition process:

1. Swab a small amount of the suspect stain with a sterile cotton swab moistened with saline.
2. Using another swab, wipe a nonstained area from an area adjacent to the suspect stain on the same surface. This is a control swab.
3. Add two drops of the testing reagent, e.g., KM reagent, onto each of the swabs.
4. Wait 30 s. If a color transformation occurs at this point in the reaction, it is indicative of a false positive associated with the presence of a strong oxidizing agent or peroxidase activity.
5. Add two drops of hydrogen peroxide (3%) to each swab.
6. Depending on the particular testing reagent, a predictable colored complex will form almost immediately to within 15 s (see Fig. M.4).

The lack of color formation is generally indicative of the absence of blood in the suspect sample. However, it is possible that chemical interferences resulted in a false negative.

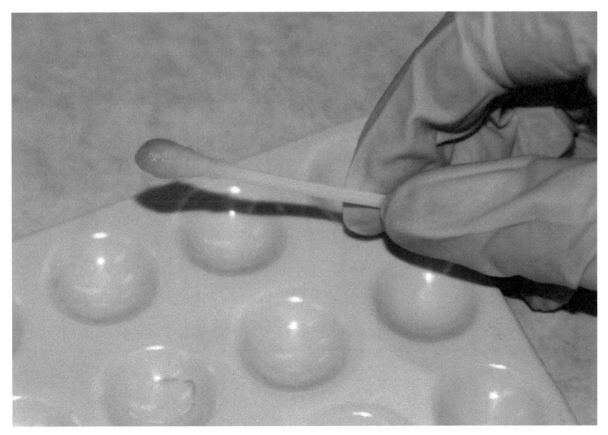

FIGURE M.4   Positive field (color) test.

Testing known blood samples at the start of an investigation is an essential way to insure the reagents are working properly.

Other Suspected Biological Evidence

Other body fluids are found at crime scenes. The more commonly encountered stains are semen, saliva, sweat, and urine. The crime scene investigator can screen for these stains with the same type of testing procedure as shown with blood. If presumptive testing indicates the presence of one or more body fluids, the remaining sample should be collected and preserved for additional laboratory testing. See Chart M.2.

1. **Semen** is a heterogeneous mixture that contains both fluid and cellular components. Many of the fluid components are amenable for detection with presumptive testing reagents. Acid phosphatase will oxidize colorless reagents to produce purple-pink color changes for screening purposes. Seminal stains can also be located and preliminarily identified by their characteristic whitish, crusty appearance and fluorescence under ultraviolet (UV) light and alternate light sources.
2. **Saliva** contains a starch-digesting enzyme, amylase. The identification of high concentrations of amylase usually indicates the presence of saliva. Sometimes the suspected area will fluoresce under examination with UV or alternate light sources.
3. **Urine** detection is based on its characteristic color and odor, as well as the presence of characteristic chemical components, such as creatinine or urea.

There are commercially available kits for detection of blood, semen, and saliva. All of the kits are self-contained and subjected to continued research on sensitivity, specificity, and reactivity.

Biological fluid	Chemical basis	Result
Semen	Acid phosphatase Flavinoids	Red-pink color UV fluorescent
Saliva	Amylase	Color change ALS fluorescent
Urine	Odor, Alkaline Creatinine	pH testing Color change
Sweat	Proteins	ALS fluorescent

CHART M.2   Field tests for other biological fluids.

LABORATORY EXERCISE

In this exercise the user will perform a series of field tests for blood, heme-based and protein staining. The exercise will illustrate the positive, negative, and false positives that may result.

Laboratory Data Sheet
Enhancement Reagents
Part A. Hemoglobin (Heme)-Based Enhancement Reagents

Luminol is frequently used as a searching or enhancement method at the crime scene. The test is based on the ability of the luminol molecule to be oxidized by the reaction of sodium perborate with an oxidizing agent such as hemoglobin (or other strong oxidizers such as iron, bleach, cleaning agents, and some foodstuffs). There are other commercially available enhancement reagents that may also be used for comparison purposes, such as Starlite Bloodhound or Blue Star.

A. Put a dilute bloodstain and a bleach solution stain on a large surface or floor area.

B. Please note that a positive control, a penny, is placed in the spray area to ensure that the reaction is occurring.

C. Put the surface in an area that can be made dark.

D. Mix together the two parts of the luminol reagent (see appendix for directions), shake, and spray the stained surface.

E. Observe any positive reactions and the intensity of the reaction.

F. Describe or draw the resulting pattern. (Photographic documentation can be practiced here, too.)

G. If other reagents are used, discuss and compare the results.

LCV can be used in place of luminol. The completely dark room is not necessary for LCV enhancement.

Part B. Protein-Reacting-Based Enhancement Reagents

Amido black is a protein-staining reagent that is commonly used for the enhancement and visualization of suspected bloodstain-patterned evidence. Its preferred use over luminol is primarily due to its sensitivity and ease of use for photographic documentation.

A. Select a piece of bloodstained brown paper.

B. Dip the paper in the amido black reagent bath for approximately 10 s.

C. Dip the paper in the "stop" reagent bath, followed by the "rinse" bath.

D. Place the paper aside to dry.

E. Is there a pattern on the brown paper?

Field Tests for Biological Evidence
Part A. Screening Tests for Blood

The combination of the KM field test with TMB will allow for an increased sensitivity of the test along with the elimination of some false positives. Use of the KM, TMB, and some false positive substances is pH dependent; therefore, by testing with the KM first, half of the potential false positives that are reacting at the pH of TMB will be eliminated. The TMB is more sensitive than KM and thus increases the sensitivity of the overall test procedure.

A. Use at least four vegetable or fruit stains, a $KMnO_4$ stain, and a known bloodstain.
B. Make swabbings of each stain by first wetting a swab with one to two drops of saline solution or distilled water. Carefully swab the specimen stain. If the fruit or vegetable is "liquidy," then you may directly swab the surface. Older stains may require repeated rubbing.

C. If one end of a cotton swab is used then the opposite end may be used as a reagent blank. Be sure to record its results as well.

D. Add one drop of 95% EtOH to each swab to clean away dirt or fat.

E. To the swab, add one drop of the KM reagent. Record the result. If a color is produced, interfering substances may be present that indicate a false positive. This is an inconclusive result.

F. Add one drop of 3% hydrogen peroxide and record the result. There should be an immediate red/pink/violet color change for a positive result. No color equals a negative result. Any other colors should be noted but considered as a negative.

G. Add one to three drops of the TMB reagent. A blue-green color is immediate and positive. No color and any other color are considered as a negative.

H. Complete the chart below.

Sample Used	EtOH	H_2O_2	KM	TMB
Known blood				
Negative control				
Potassium permanganate				

Part B. Screening Tests for Other Biological Fluids: Semen and Saliva

While there are many commercially available "kits" to assist with the screening of possible seminal and saliva stains, using an ALS or UV (black) light remains the easiest to use and interpret. Blue-white fluorescence is a presumptive positive reaction. Several light-colored fabrics may obscure the observation. For this reason, the color-test reactions may need to be run after the light searching.

1. Prepare neat saliva and seminal stains on a variety of fabrics. Be sure to include a white background fabric. Allow the stains to dry.
2. Observe the stains with either an UV or an ALS set to the blue-light setting. Did you observe any background interferences? What was the background color?
3. Prepare the following diluted stains (fluid:saline): 1:10, 1:100, 1:1000, and 1:2500. Use the background fabric that produced the best result in step 2. Allow the stains to dry.
4. Observe the diluted stains using the UV or ALS. Are all of the diluted stains seen? What is the maximum dilution observed?

5. Complete the data chart below. A+ indicates that fluorescence was observed:

Sample Used	Fabric #1	Fabric #2	Fabric #3	Fabric #4
Neat semen				
Neat saliva				
1: 10 semen				
1: 100 semen				
1: 1000 semen				
1: 2500 semen				
1: 10 saliva				
1: 100 saliva				
1: 1000 saliva				
1: 2500 saliva				

DISCUSSION QUESTIONS

1. What were the difficulties encountered when using and documenting the luminol-enhanced blood pattern? How would you overcome these difficulties?

2. What types of situations would require spraying with a protein-reacting enhancement reagent versus using immersion techniques?

3. The heme-based field tests are very sensitive. Why is this an advantage in crime scene investigations?

4. If you have enhanced a suspected bloodstain pattern with a protein-staining reagent, is it necessary to perform a blood field test? Why or why not?

5. What were some of the fruits, vegetables, or other substrates that gave false positive results with the KM and TMB reagents?

Exercise N

Visualization and Enhancement: Chemical Evidence

This exercise covers presumptive and identity testing of gunshot residue (GSR), explosives, controlled substances, and other chemical-based physical evidence.

Learning Objectives

- To understand and apply the use of field or color tests as a means for searching and screening for various types of chemical physical evidence at a mock crime scene.

The same searching and screening principles used with biological evidence can be applied to a variety of chemical substances. The purpose of the screening or enhancement procedures is to facilitate the crime scene investigator's search for these oftentimes-trace amounts of physical evidence. This exercise will include three types of chemical evidence: GSR, explosive residues, and controlled substances or drugs.

TESTS FOR GUNSHOT RESIDUE

When a firearm is discharged, it creates gases, soot, and burned or partially burned gunpowder particles that are deposited on any surface at the crime scene, especially on the shooter's hand and the intended target. GSR comes from detonation of the primer, gunpowder, lubricants, or

Crime Scene Investigation Laboratory Manual, Second Edition
http://dx.doi.org/10.1016/B978-0-12-812845-9.00014-5

components of the projectile. These materials are propelled forward with the projectile toward the target and on the surfaces of any nearby objects. Searching for GSR may aid in identification of the shooter and help locate those areas in which additional samples should be collected for laboratory analysis. GSR evidence can also be used as pattern evidence to determine the range of fire or target to muzzle distances.

The components of GSR are shown in Chart N.1.

Gunshot Residue Tests

Detection of GSR has two primary objectives: (1) determining if an individual fired or handled a recently discharged firearm or if a surface was in close proximity to a weapon

CHART N.1   Gunshot Residue Components

PRIMER RESIDUES:

• Explosives:	Lead styphnate
	Lead azide
	Diaz odinitro phenol
• Oxidizing Agents:	Barium nitrate
	Calcium peroxide
	Magnesium peroxide
	Magnesium dioxide
• Fuels:	Antimony sulfide
	Calcium silicide
	Aluminum
	Titanium
	Zirconium
	Lead thiocyanate
• Sensitizing Agents:	Tetracene
	Powdered glass
	Titanium
	Calcium silicide

GUN POWDER:

• Smokeless:	Nitrocellulose
	Nitrocellulose with nitroglycerine
• Black:	Potassium nitrate
	Sulfur
	Charcoal

LUBRICANTS

Projectile Components:

• **Lead, copper, zinc, antimony, arsenic, bismuth, and chromium**

during discharge; and (2) analyzing the pattern of GSR for the purpose of determining the muzzle-to-target distance. Any test designed to detect GSR must be used in a manner that minimizes the potential for damaging or changing the GSR pattern. Like other presumptive or screening tests, the color tests suitable for detection of GSR at crime scenes must be confirmed by more precise laboratory testing.

Gunshot Residue Test Reagents

These reagents react with nitrate and nitrite compounds in GSR, yielding a colored reaction for preliminary identification or for pattern enhance for range of fire determination. Reagents can be used as swabbed color tests or by a spraying application. Commonly occurring substances such as cigarette smoke, urine, and fertilizer may sometimes also react with these reagents.

TESTS FOR EXPLOSIVE RESIDUES

Explosive residues may be encountered in numerous forms at the scene. Explosive residues may be located on the hands or clothes of a suspect, at storage or production sites, and in vehicles or containers used to transport explosive material. At postblast scenes, these residues may consist of both unchanged explosive material and the products of the explosion.

Explosives are chemical substances that can be stable or unstable in their natural forms. When heated, shocked, or ignited, they are capable of rapid breakdown, producing an explosion by the liberation of large quantities of heat and gas. Explosives are classified into three primary categories, shown in Chart N.2.

Field Tests for Explosive Materials

Portable hydrocarbon or ion "sniffers" can be used for detecting explosive residues on objects or persons at crime scenes. Canine programs have reported significant success

CHART N.2   Explosives Categories

Category	Characteristics	Examples
Low explosive	Burners: must be confined	Gunpowder Fireworks
Primary high explosive	Sensitive to friction or shock	Blasting caps Detonation cord Nitroglycerine
Secondary high explosive	Main charges: require detonation	Dynamite TNT RDX C-4 Ammonium nitrate

detecting minute amounts of explosive materials. Also, there are various color reagents that give characteristic colors when the suspect sample is tested. Instrumental and noninstrumental methods are always evolving as the need for identification of trace explosive materials is required in these post-9/11 days. As shown with the biological evidence presumptive tests, both false negatives and false positives are possible. Therefore, laboratory confirmatory testing is essential.

Explosive Test Reagents

These reagents react with nitrate and nitrite compounds found in all three categories of explosives to produce color reactions. As with the GSR, these reagents can be used as swabbed color tests or through a spraying application. Of course, all presumptive field tests locate possible evidence to be collected for lab confirmation. Remember that the results of these tests are part of a searching process at the crime scene, and the results indicate whether the sample should be collected for submission to the forensic laboratory.

TESTS FOR CONTROLLED SUBSTANCES AND DRUGS

Crime scenes are often part of drug investigations such as the investigation of clandestine labs or other crimes relating to drug cases. As such, crime scene investigators may be asked to search the scenes for controlled substances on a variety of surfaces. Therefore, there is often a need for a quick screening test or field test to analyze a material suspected of being a drug or controlled substance. In many situations, these field tests help provide the necessary probable cause to substantiate an arrest for sale and/or possession of a controlled substance.

Color tests are very common, used often, and are widely accepted as screening tests in drug analysis.

Field Tests for Drug Substances

Certain drugs will react with selected chemical reagents to give characteristic color changes or precipitates. Easy-to-use kits with widespread use that contain these reagents in convenient single-test vials are commercially available. Some commonly used drug-screening reagents and their characteristic reactions are shown in Chart N.3.

Drug Test Reagents

Because there are hundreds of controlled substances, screening tests are performed to narrow the possible choices of an unknown. Adding a reagent to a small amount of the sample and observing any reaction—a color change, a precipitate formation, or the production of a gas, is the technique for perform the test. The results of the screening technique will be used to determine if a sample should be collected from the crime scene. The specific color test used is information that the laboratory can find useful to help determine what technique will be used to positively identify the controlled substance.

CHART N.3   Field Test for Drug Substances

Reagent	Application	Result
Marquis	Large variety: general reagent	Opiates = purple PCP = colorless to light pink Phenethlamines = orange to brown LSD = orange/brown/purple Mescaline and psilocybin = orange
Mandelin	Variety: phenethylamines	Opiates = blue-gray Ampethamines = green LSD = orange/green/gray Psilocybin = green
Conc. nitric acid	Morphine versus heroin	Morphine = orange to red Heroin = yellow to green
Duquenois	Marihuana; Tetrahydrocannabinol (THC)	Marihuana, Tetrahydrocannabinol (THC), and hashish = blue-violet
Cobalt thiocyanate	Cocaine and derivatives	"Cocaines" = blue precipitate
Dille–Koppanyi	Barbiturates	Red-violet

LABORATORY EXERCISE

Fore these exercises gloves and a testing location with an exhaust fan or laboratory hood is essential. Some of the reagents may produce a vigorous reaction. Care is urged. The reagent recipes are found in the Appendix.

Laboratory Data Sheet

Explosives Test Reagents Test Procedures

For this part of the exercise, known and unknown GSR samples will be necessary for testing. It is best to use a variety of surfaces as well. A good resource is a local shooting range to prepare or obtain samples. Use all the testing reagents for this exercise.

Part A. Diphenylamine

This reagent reacts with nitrate and nitrite components of GSR.

1. Swab the area to be tested with a cotton swab moistened with distilled water.
2. Add a drop of DPA in a sulfuric acid solution. STRONG ACID!
3. The immediate development of a dark blue color indicates the presence of nitrates/nitrites.

Part B. Modified Greiss Test

This reagent reacts with nitrite components of GSR.

1. Process desensitized photographic paper with a mixture of 50% alpha-naphthol solution and 50% sulfanilic acid solution; allow paper to dry.
2. Place the evidence item, questioned side down, on the gelatin-coated side of the treated photographic paper.
3. Place a piece of cloth soaked in 15% glacial acetic acid solution on the questioned item, and press with a hot iron.
4. Any orange indications on the photographic paper are the result of a color-producing reaction specific for the presence of nitrite residues.

Part C. Sodium Rhodizonate Test

This reagent is a specific color test for lead in GSR.

1. Spray the questioned surface with a saturated solution of sodium rhodizonate in distilled water.
2. Spray the same area with the tartaric acid/sodium bitartrate buffer solution.
3. Spray the same area with a 5% hydrochloric acid solution.
4. The previous pink color will fade out, and the blue-violet area constitutes a positive reaction for lead. Prompt note-taking is essential because a positive result may fade.

Explosive Residues Test Procedures

For this part of the exercise, the following samples will be needed for testing with Griess reagent, diphenylamine, methylene blue, and alcoholic potassium hydroxide:

Zinc chloride
Sodium carbonate
Nitrocellulose
Sodium nitrite
Potassium perchlorate
Sodium chloride
Potassium iodide
Lead nitrate
Sodium bromide
Sodium sulfate

Use the flat end of a toothpick to sample the above substances. Place the samples on a spot plate or glass microscope slide. Sometimes a black background helps to see the reactions. A datasheet of the samples and reagents will help to visually compare the results.

Part A. Griess Reagent

This is a color test for the presence of nitrates, nitrites, and nitro compounds.

1. Add one drop of Griess I to each sample in the spot plate.
2. Observe any change in color.
3. Add Griess II to the same well, and note any color change.
4. The appearance of a red color fading immediately to yellow indicates a strong inorganic nitrite reaction. If no color develops, add a few grains of washed, powdered zinc. The development of a red color indicates the presence of nitrates, nitrites, or organic nitro compounds.

Part B. Diphenylamine

This is a color test for the presence of nitrates or nitrites. Use caution! This reagent contains *concentrated sulfuric acid* (H_2SO_4). STRONG ACID!

1. Add one drop of DPA to each of the samples.
2. Note the color of the reaction.
3. The immediate development of a dark blue color indicates the presence of nitrates/nitrites.

Part C. Methylene Blue

This is a color test for the presence of strong oxidizing chemicals.

1. Add one drop of Solution 1 to the samples. Observe any color change.
2. Add one drop of Solution 2 to the same well. The reaction may produce both a color change and a precipitate.

Part D. Alcoholic Potassium Hydroxide (alc. KOH)

This is primarily a test for TNT (not provided to the student!) and similar compounds.

1. Add one drop of alcoholic KOH to the samples.
2. Observe any reaction.

Tests for Controlled Substances and Drug Procedures

For this exercise, a variety of drug substances or known chemicals will be used for the color reagents shown below. The color reagents commonly contain concentrated sulfuric acid, so use caution; protective eyewear is essential. Suggested reagents:

> Concentrated nitric acid (STRONG ACID!)
> Dille–Koppanyi reagent (D-K)
> Marquis reagent (STRONG ACID!)
> Mandelin reagent (STRONG ACID!)
> Cobalt thiocyanate (CoSCN)

Suggested knowns (this list includes some controlled substances that require a DEA license):

> Codeine
> Allergy pill (ephedrine)
> Cocaine
> Aspirin (acetylsalicylic acid, ASA)
> Phenobarbital
> Tylenol (acetaminophen, APAP)
> Amphetamine
> Dramamine (diphenhydramine)
> Lidocaine

1. Using clean spot plates and the flat end of a toothpick, set up the spot plates according to the following table, using small amounts of the sample to be tested.

	Concentrated Nitric Acid	Marquis	CoSCN	Mandelin	Dille–Koppanyi Reagent
Codeine					
Cocaine					
Phenolbarb					
Amphetamine					
Lidocaine					
Ephedrine					
Aspirin					
Tylenol					
Dramamine					

2. Carefully:

    a. Add one drop of nitric acid to the knowns and unknown.

    b. Repeat with the Marquis reagent.

    c. Repeat with the CoSCN reagent.

    d. Repeat with the Mandelin reagent.

    e. Repeat with the Dille–Koppanyi reagent.

    f. Record the results in the table.

DISCUSSION QUESTIONS

1. For the color reagents for GSR, explosive residues, and drug substances, what is the significance of a positive result for the crime scene investigator?

2. What is the significance of a negative result with these color reagents?

3. What must the crime scene investigator do before any of these reagents are used at the crime scene?

4. Why is it that many of the same color reagents for testing for GSR are used for testing of explosive residues?

Exercise O

Visualization and Enhancement: Impressions

Learning Objectives

- To define the three types of impression evidence: imprints, indentations, and striations.
- To identify and apply the techniques of visualization of impressions found on a variety of surfaces, such as: nonporous, porous, bloody, wet, sticky, etc.

In previous exercises, several methods have been used to search for physical evidence at crime scenes. Exercise L used various light sources, and Exercises M and N used the chemical reactivity of biological and chemical evidence as a basis for searching for evidence. In this exercise, a combination of all of these methods will be used to search for and enhance impression evidence, especially fingerprints, based on the type of surface on which the impression has been deposited or made.

IMPRESSION EVIDENCE

Impression evidence is created when two surfaces are in contact. The impression is a transfer of material or is made when one surface is harder than the other surface it contacts. The three categories of impression evidence are shown in Fig. O.1.

Impression Type	Mechanism	Examples
Imprint	2-D; transfer of materials from one surface to another surface	Patent and latent fingerprints
Indentation	3-D; one surface harder than the other softer surface that forms the shape of the harder surface	Footwear in snow, mud, firing pin impression
Striation	Indentation with motion or sliding movement	Tool or prymarks, barrel marks on fired projectiles

FIGURE O.1   Types of impressions.

It is the task of the crime scene investigator to search for, enhance, and document impression evidence. Collection and preservation are discussed in subsequent exercises.

Imprint Evidence

This type of impression evidence is created when material from one surface is transferred to another surface. A two-dimensional pattern results from the material transferred. Example imprints can be blood, dust, mud, paint, or just about anything—easily seen or not! Patent (visible) or latent (difficult to see or "invisible") fingerprints are of this type of impression. Patent imprints require no enhancement but must be carefully photographed prior to collection. Latent imprints require enhancement. The type of enhancement is dependent on the type of material transferred, along with the nature of the surface on which the imprint was deposited. Fig. O.2 summarizes the enhancement methods for imprints.

Indentation and Striations Evidence

An indentation type of impression evidence occurs when two surfaces contact, and one surface is harder than the other, softer surface. The three-dimensional shape or pattern of the harder surface will be "impressed" on the resulting softer surface. Examples of this type of indentation are footwear patterns in snow or mud, fingerprints in semiwet paint (often called a "plastic" fingerprint), or even a drag mark through sand or soil. Striations are indentations with motion. Toolmarks and the impressions on fired projectiles are good examples of striation-containing evidence. There are no enhancement reagents for indentation and striation impressions.

Reagent use:

Blood enhancement:	Amido black
	Coomassie blue
	Crowle's double stain
	DAB
	Fluorescein
	Leucocrystal violet
	Luminol
Latent prints:	Powder dusting
	Ninhydrin
	Superglue (hotshots, cyanowand, pouches)
	Sticky Surface Powder
	DFO
	Small Particle Reagent
	Ardrox
	Rhodamine 6G

FIGURE O.2   Imprint enhancement.

Enhancement of Impression Evidence: Combination Methods With Alternate Light Source

Fig. O.2 summarizes the various methods for the enhancement of impression evidence. Special methods of enhancement sometimes utilize a combination of alternate light sources (ALSs) with physical and chemical techniques. These combination methods are especially useful for latent fingerprints and bloodstain patterns. The enhancement reagents chosen are based on their chemical composition and the chemical reactions that occur when reacting with the various types of patterned impression evidence. As shown in previous exercises, to enhance **bloodstain patterns**, most reagents are oxidation-reduction reactions with hemoglobin or proteins found in blood. All the blood-enhancement reagents will not interfere with subsequent DNA analysis if used properly. The enhancement reagents for **latent fingerprint** enhancement react with chemicals found in the residues deposited on various surfaces.

IV. PHYSICAL EVIDENCE AT CRIME SCENES

LABORATORY EXERCISE

For this exercise the user will visualize a variety of fingerprint impressions. The method used for visualization will be dependent on the surface that "holds" the impression.

Laboratory Data Sheet

Part A. Latent Fingerprints on a Nonporous Surface
Powder Dusting

For this part of the exercise, select any nonporous surface and place a fingerprint on it. At least three different samples will be needed.

1. Using a brush of your choice, feather or polyester, carefully dust the surface using black powder.
2. Tape-lift the developed latent.
3. Transfer the lift to a backing card with appropriate documentation (see Fig. O.3).
4. Repeat these steps using magnetic powder and fluorescent powder (view the developed latent using the UV lamp).

Sticky Surface Dusting

This technique will enhance fingerprints found on sticky surfaces such as the adhesive side of duct tape. The reagent is a paste of black powder in water that is brushed on to the adhesive side of tape surfaces. Superglue fuming will not interfere with this technique. This technique is more economical and user-friendly than other techniques. Prepare samples using sections of precut duct tape.

1. Put one teaspoon of powder in a shallow jar. Add equal parts of dish detergent or Photo-Flo and water to the powder to make a paste.
2. Brush the paste onto the sticky surface.
3. Wait 1 min. Rinse the surface with a gentle stream of cold water. Allow to dry.
4. Tape lifting can be attempted as well (see Fig. O.4).

Part B. Latent Fingerprints on a Porous Surface
Physical Enhancement: Gel Lifters

Gelatin lifters are specially developed for the lifting of fingerprints, other imprints, and microtrace evidence from porous surfaces. The lifter's thick, nonaggressive, lowadhesive gelatin layer permits the lifting of imprints and trace evidence from almost every surface. The lifter consists of three layers: the carrier, the gelatin adhesive, and the cover sheet. Black and white gel lifters are available.

1. Prepare dust shoe imprints on manila file folders.
2. Before lifting the impression, cut off a small corner of the lifter. This will insure that the cover sheet will always be properly replaced and will also insure proper orientation of the impression on the lifter.

FIGURE O.3   Magnetic powder dusting of a nonporous surface.

IV. PHYSICAL EVIDENCE AT CRIME SCENES

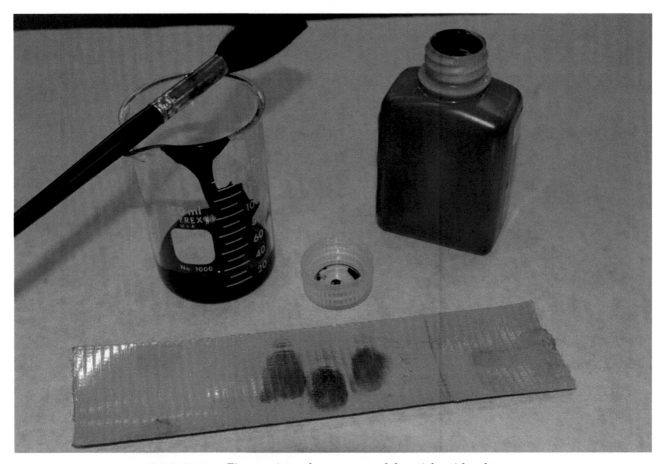

FIGURE O.4   Fingerprint enhancement of the sticky side of tape.

3. Remove the cover sheet from the lifter and place it safely aside.
4. Lift the impression. To do this, adhere to an edge of the lifter to a side of the impression. Carefully smooth down the remaining portion of the lifter over the impression so that no air bubbles result.
5. Beginning at one of the lifter's corners, pick up the lifter and place it on the bench top (flat, horizontal surface). Replace the cover sheet using a technique similar to the lifting procedure. For larger impressions, a roller may be used. Take care not to put so much pressure on the lifter as to cause distortions of the impression. See Fig. O.5.

Physical Enhancement: Electrostatic Lifter

Dust imprints on porous surfaces can be lifted by passing an electric current through the imprint and forcing the imprint onto a mylar metallic sheet.

1. Obtain the imprint sample on the same porous surface as before.
2. Cut the metallic sheeting to fit the imprint size.
3. Following the instructions of the electrostatic lifter, lift, or transfer the imprint from its porous surface. See Fig. O.6.
4. Once the imprint is on the metallic sheeting, package it properly.

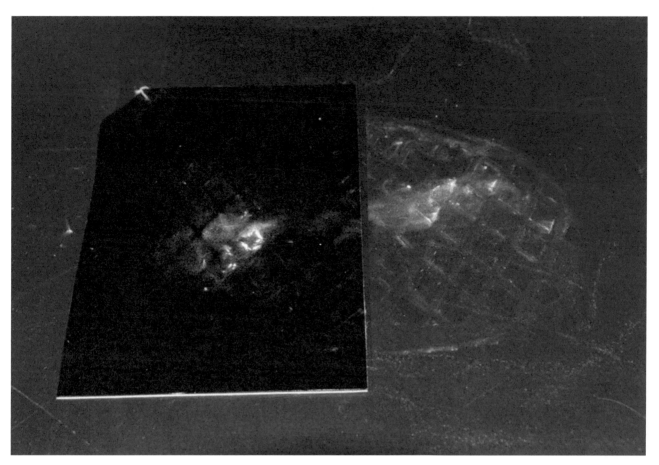

FIGURE O.5   Gel lifter imprints on porous surfaces.

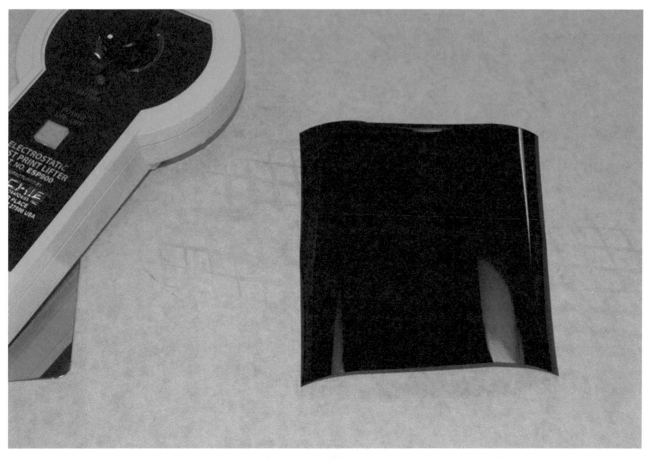

FIGURE O.6   Using an electrostatic lifter; imprints on porous surfaces.

Chemical Enhancement: Protein Staining = Ninhydrin

This part of the exercise will require fingerprints to be placed on pieces of paper. Try making stains 24 h before analysis and stains that are within 1 h of testing.

1. In the hood, use the sprayer unit with the ninhydrin to moisten the paper to soaking.
2. Place the paper in an 80 degree oven for 10 min, heat with a hair dryer, or allow the ninhydrin solution to dry overnight.
3. A purple-violet pattern will appear. See Fig. O.7.

Chemical Enhancement: Protein Staining = Amido Black

As before, use paper as the surface, but stain the paper with very dilute blood-stained fingerprints. Be sure to allow the imprints to dry overnight. This is a spraying technique.

1. Spray with dye solution (2 g amido black, 100 mL glacial acetic acid, and 900 mL methanol) for 30–90 s.
2. Apply the rinse solution (100 mL glacial acetic acid and 900 mL methanol).
3. Rinse with a final wash of dH$_2$O.
4. The blood will stain to a deep blue to black color. See Fig. O.8.

Part C. Combination Methods of Enhancement of Various Surfaces

Chemical Enhancement: Wet Surfaces = Small Particle Reagent

This is a chemical technique used for wet surfaces, both porous and nonporous. It can be messy. This reagent can be used after supergluing if other techniques are ineffective. Enhanced detail is photographed and sometimes lifted depending on the surface type. The reagent is a water-based solution with molybdenum disulfide. There is no need to dry the surface before application.

1. Spray the item with the reagent. Shake bottle and reapply.
2. Rinse with tap water.
3. Allow the surface to dry. Photograph the dark-colored friction ridges or lift.

"Combination" Enhancement: Cyanoacrylate (Superglue) Fuming and Powder Dusting

Cyanoacrylate (superglue) self-polymerizes on exposure to the air. This polymer will coat surfaces with latent fingerprints so that they can then be powder-dusted. Portable fuming tanks can be transported to crime scenes for processing there; larger fixed tanks in laboratories are useful as well.

1. Use a soda can, a piece of a plastic baggie, or a microscope slide with a latent applied in a glass tank (aquariums work well).
2. Process by fuming with superglue. There are lots of commercial products available, but a few drops of superglue on a mug warmer works. A small beaker with warm water (humidity) helps dispense the fumes! See Fig. O.9.

FIGURE O.7 Enhancing latent fingerprints on paper with protein stain ninhydrin: (A) spraying and (B) heating.

FIGURE O.8   Enhancing a faint bloodstained-footwear impression with protein stain amido black.

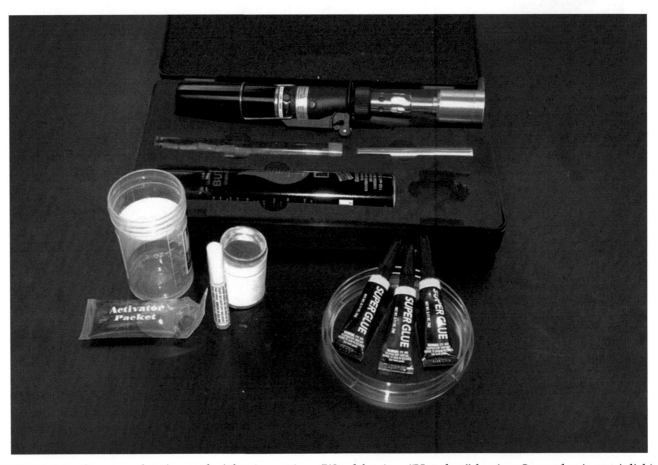

FIGURE O.9   Cyanoacrylate (superglue) fuming options (Wand fuming, "Hot-shot" fuming, Superglue in petri dish).

3. Allow the cyanoacrylate fumes to coat the latent for 10–15 min. It is a good idea to use a known latent on a similar surface to run with the scene evidence.
4. Once the latent has been developed, dust with black or magnetic powder, and lift the latent to a backing card.

Combination Method: A Variety of Methods With Alternate Light Source

1,8-Diazafluoren-9-one   The chemical enhancement is a reaction of the amino acids and eccrine compounds of latent prints. It works for porous surfaces prior to ninhydrin spraying. It is viewed using a red filter and an ALS at 495–550 nm.

1. Spray the item with the 1,8-diazafluoren-9-one (DFO) working solution (1 g DFO crystals, 200 mL MeOH, 200 mL ethyl acetate, 40 mL glacial acetic acid, and add petroleum ether [or pentane] to 2 L). Air dry in hood.
2. Respray a second time. Air dry in hood.
3. Heat in oven (80°C) for 15 min, or heat dry with hair dryer.
4. View with an ALS with a yellow color barrier filter.

Ardrox Processing   This is a fluorescent-dye-staining technique used to make superglue-developed latents more visible with UV and an ALS (435–480 nm) and yellow filter.

1. The surface is sprayed or dipped in the Ardrox working solution (commercially prepared is easiest and cheap).
2. Water rinse.
3. View with ALS. Photograph.

Rhodiamine 6G Processing   Similar to the Ardrox process, but use ALS at 495–550 nm with a red filter.

1. Spray with the solution (commercial solutions are best).
2. View with ALS and photograph. See Fig. O.10.

Part D. Enhancement of Indentations (Striations)

Indentations are enhanced and ultimately collected by "casting" the pattern impressed on the soft surface.

Dental Stone Casting

Dental stone casting material, a form of gypsum, is used for tire tread and footwear indentations found at the crime scene. The cast provides a lifelike, actual-size reproduction of the original impression that includes uneven surfaces, microscopic characteristics, and characteristics of the outer- and midsoles of the shoe or tire. Plaster of Paris is not used as it shrinks on drying. Some polymeric casting materials are also used.

1. Make your own indentations. Assume that the impression to be cast has been properly photographed. Remove any large, loose pieces of foreign matter without disturbing the impression.
2. Prepare the impression for casting by coating it with hair spray. This process should be carefully done so as not to disturb the impression.

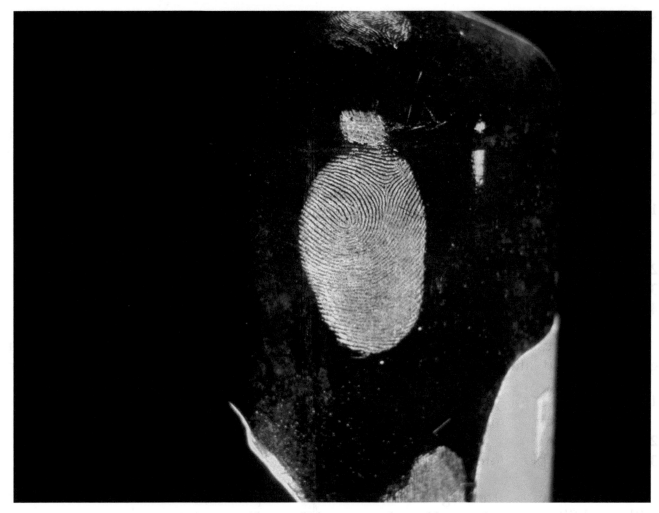

FIGURE O.10   Alternate light source–enhanced latent print.

3. Using a rubber mixing bowl, prepare the mixture. To do this, add about seven ounces of water to the bowl, and then gradually add the dental stone material *while stirring*. (A "pancake batter" consistency is preferred.)
4. Pour roughly half of the mixture onto the impression while deflecting the mixture flow with a spoon or spatula. Continue pouring to a depth of about half an inch. See Fig. O.11.
5. Place reinforcement materials on the top of the layer. Reinforcement materials include screen, wire, rods, etc.
6. Pour another layer with the remaining half of the dental stone mixture on the top of the reinforcement materials.
7. Before the cast has hardened, scratch any necessary identifying information into the surface (name, date, etc.).
8. Allow the cast to completely harden. Carefully lift the cast to a sturdy surface for packaging (you may rinse it with water to remove any excess dirt or debris before packaging).

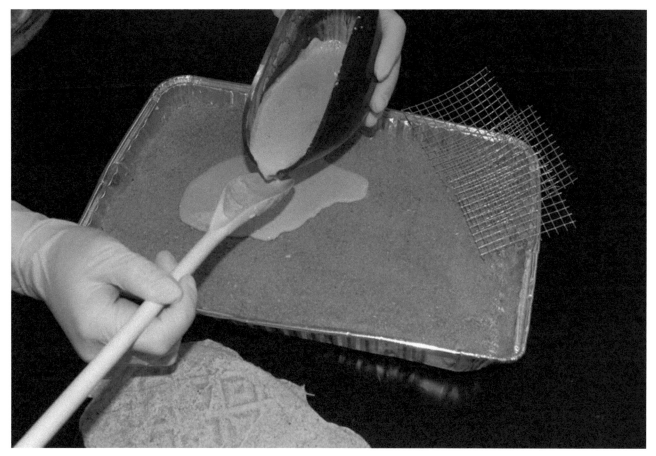

FIGURE O.11   Dental stone casting of a footwear indentation.

Silicone Casting

This casting technique allows for the enhancement of finely sized indentations such as plastic fingerprints or striations such as toolmarks. The casting materials are polymers that frequently require a two-step process involving a hardening agent. Many commercial products are available.

1. Prepare a toolmark on a piece of lead (or other soft metal).
2. Apply the casting materials. Allow to set up. See Fig. O.12.
3. Lift the silicone cast.

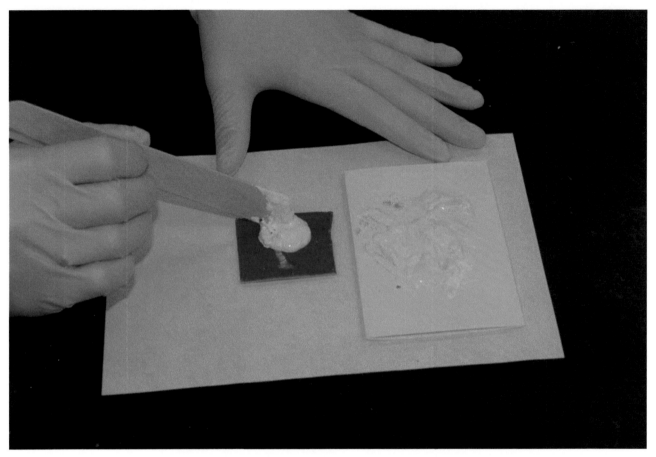

FIGURE O.12   Silicone casting of a toolmark impression.

DISCUSSION QUESTIONS

1. What are other chemical-staining reagents that are used for enhancing latent fingerprints with the use of an ALS? Additional research may be necessary; why?

2. Why is a print developed with ninhydrin sometimes only viable for a certain period? Hint: This involves the type of surface.

3. Why is it a good idea to use a penny as a control with luminol and other heme-based enhancement reagents? If as part of your enhancement efforts at the crime scene you recorded a false positive, why could this result have occurred? Do not just use circumstantial information; utilize chemical makeup and reaction reasoning as well.

4. Name two advantages and two disadvantages to using amido black at the crime scene.

5. Silicone casts for toolmark striations are very flexible and flimsy. How should these casts be protected so they are not damaged when collected? What about dental stone casts?

Exercise P

Packaging, Preservation, and Collection of Evidence

Learning Objectives

- To learn and combine proper searching techniques with proper packaging, preserving, and collecting evidence at the crime scene.
- To identify and use a variety of containers for packaging, preserving, and collecting evidence at the crime scene.
- To use and apply basic guidelines for the packaging, preserving, and collecting evidence at the crime scene.
- To practice folding druggist folds for use as primary containers.

After the completion of the crime scene documentation and the science-based, systematic search of the crime scene for physical evidence, the evidence must be collected and taken from the scene using proper techniques for preservation. One person is designated as the evidence officer so that all evidence is collected, packaged, marked, sealed, and preserved in a consistent manner. The single collector assures that the relevancy, reliability, and validity of the physical evidence is maintained and not called into question at any stage of the investigation.

There is no set order for the collection of evidence, but some general guidelines for evidence collection are summarized in Fig. P.1.

If any fragile, easily lost, or transient evidence has been identified during any stage of the scene investigation, it should be collected first. Each item of physical evidence must be collected and packaged separately to prevent any cross-contamination between items of evidence. The packages must also be closed and sealed at the time of collection. This procedure will ensure that no intermingling of the physical evidence will occur during transportation.

Crime Scene Investigation Laboratory Manual, Second Edition
http://dx.doi.org/10.1016/B978-0-12-812845-9.00016-9

- If wet, allow to dry.

- If moveable, be sure it is documented, then collect in its entirety.

- If immoveable, collect off surface properly, and be sure to collect controls.

- Collect/package in a primary container followed by a secondary container.

- Use *no* airtight containers!

- Mark, seal, initial, date, and describe (MSIDD) at the scene.

- Use universal precautions always.

FIGURE P.1   General guidelines for collection and packaging.

Most physical evidence will be collected into a primary container or druggist's fold and placed into a secondary container or outer container. This "packaging sequence" will protect the evidence from loss or alteration (breaking, marring, or changes) and assure the reliability of intact or preserved evidence. Druggist's folds are typically used for small trace evidence, but they are also useful for protecting items of evidence of any size that may "hold" trace evidence that will need to be collected by the crime scene investigator or laboratory personnel at a later time. Outer containers can be boxes, envelopes, paper bags, or canisters. The outer containers are sealed with evidence tape that completely covers any openings. The seals are marked with documentation information about the item of evidence, the identity of the collector, the date, time, location where the evidence was collected, the agency case number, and a brief description of the physical evidence, with its location contained within the secondary container. See Fig. P.2 for the sealing and marking process.

Most physical evidence is solid and can easily be packaged, stored, and preserved in the previously noted containers. If the physical evidence is volatile or easily lost due to evaporation, airtight containers such as metal paint cans, jars, and specially designed bags are to be used for packaging. Liquid items of physical evidence can be packaged and transported in unbreakable, leakproof containers. Moist, wet, or biological evidence (blood, suspected marihuana plants, etc.) collected by methods described further ahead can temporarily be packaged as described previously; later, in a controlled drying area, they can

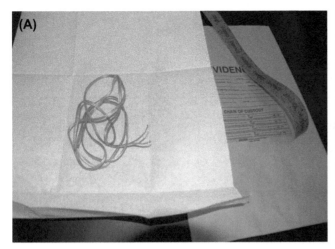
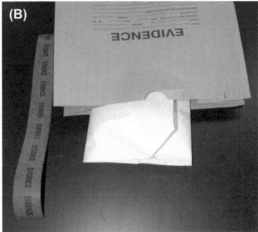

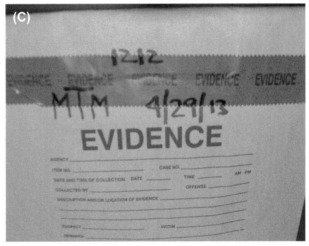

FIGURE P.2 Packaging, sealing, and marking evidence. (A) Evidence before packaging. (B) Primary container into secondary container. (C) Sealed and marked packaging.

be allowed to air dry and can be repackaged into nonairtight containers. The original, temporary packages must be retained and packaged with the evidence.

Finally, the crime scene investigator must always keep in mind that all physical evidence is important to the criminal investigation and should be collected. Forensic laboratory analytical techniques are constantly improving, the amount of sample required for testing has been reduced, and the identification and individualization information about the probable sources of the evidence has significantly improved. Because of the improving forensic laboratory techniques and sensitivities, the proper collection and packaging of physical evidence is *extremely* important. Advanced techniques in the laboratory cannot be used if the evidence is lost or contaminated because of improper or poor collection and packaging at the crime scene.

Some of the basic collection and preservation techniques for broad groups of evidence are shown in Fig. P.3.

Category	Photo	Lifted	Cast	Collect from surface	1°	2°	Controls
Imprints	X, EQP	X				X	Elimination prints
Indentations	X, EQP		Dental Stone		X	X	Possible sources
Striations	X, EQP		Silicone Rubber		X	X	Possible sources
Trace	X	Tape, Gel		X	X	X	Possible sources
Hair	X			X	X	X	Possible sources
Fibers	X			X	X	X	Possible sources
Glass	X			X	X	X	Possible sources
Paint	X			X	X	X	Possible sources
Firearms	X				X	X	
Gunshot residue	X			X	X	X	
Physiological fluids	X, EQP			X	X	X	Possible sources
Accelerants	X					X, airtight	Possible sources
Drugs	X				X	X	
Explosive residues	X			X	X	X	
Questioned documents	x				X	X, Window envelopes	Possible sources

FIGURE P.3   Categories of physical evidence with packaging and preservation methods.

LABORATORY EXERCISE

For this exercise the user will learn to fold a druggist fold and, based on some suggested scenarios, combine searching, visualizations, and enhancement with packaging and collection.

Laboratory Data Sheet

Part One: Preparing a Druggist Fold (Primary Container)

For this exercise a piece of trace evidence is needed. A paper clip can work! The druggist fold will be folded using a 4×5 piece of tracing paper or glassine weighing paper.

Folding the Paper

1. Using a portrait orientation, bring the bottom edge of the paper to within a half inch (~1 cm) of the top edge. Crease it.
2. Take the top edge and bring it down over the lower edge just folded.
3. Repeat step 2 for a doubled fold.
4. Put the paper on a flat surface and horizontally orient the paper. Bring the left edge one-third of the way towards the right side. Crease it and return it to the original flat position.
5. Repeat step 4, bringing the right edge to the left side.
6. Open up the folded paper, place the item of evidence (paper clip) in the center of the creases, and repeat steps 1–5.
7. One of the edges should be shorter in length than the other edge. Using the shorter edge, stuff it inside the longer edge.
8. The folded druggist fold you created should be complete at this point. Druggist folds folded this way can be small or large depending on the size of the evidence.

Part Two: Combining Searching with Collection

Thus far, many different types of physical evidence from crime scenes have been discussed. You know how to document it, search for it, and how to collect it. Use your skills to complete the following tasks for each of the scenarios ahead:

- Identify the type of evidence; be specific here.
- Describe the type of evidence (fingerprint, hair, etc.), the type/porosity of the surface it's on, and if there are any details that should be included in the description to help dictate how it should be treated.
- Discuss enhancement/visualization and searching techniques. Describe what can be done at the scene and then what you would expect to be done in the laboratory.
- Identify presumptive or screening tests that are appropriate. Describe what can be done at the scene and what you would expect to be done in the laboratory. Sometimes these tests may not be necessary.
- Describe how you would collect and package the evidence at the scene to preserve it so as to arrive safely and completely to a secure location or the laboratory. The type of packaging (paper, plastic, cardboard box, etc.) is sufficient for packaging purposes.

Evidence Scenarios

1. A cash register receipt handled by a robbery suspect
2. A colt .38 special revolver taken from a suspect of a fatal shooting
3. Dusty footwear imprints on a piece of paper shopping bag found next to the victim
4. Latent fingerprints on a suicide note found next to the victim
5. Patent or visible fingerprints on the sticky side of some duct tape
6. Red stains on the carpet at a burglary
7. Suspect latent fingerprints on the black plastic drawer of the cash register stolen from a 7–11 store
8. Suspect paint scrapings on a highway guardrail near the scene of a hit and run investigation
9. Suspect latent fingerprints on a body that was found at a secondary crime scene
10. Suspect latent fingerprints on a tinted plate glass window of a store that has been burglarized
11. Suspect trace evidence found in a police car's backseat after a suspect has been transported to jail
12. Tire-tread impression in snow next to the body at a crime scene on a sunny day
13. Unknown fibers on a homicide victim's body
14. White powdered substance on the surface of a rolled $20 bill taken from a drug dealer
15. A burned section of carpet from the living room of the scene of a house fire (the fire marshal is present at the scene)

DISCUSSION QUESTIONS

1. What do you do at a crime scene if the moveable item to be collected is larger than any of the boxes you have for packaging?

2. Is it appropriate for the team of crime scene investigators to enhance or visualize the evidence for the evidence collector? Why or why not?

3. Once evidence is sealed, how would you open the packaging to process or reprocess the evidence? How would you seal the evidence after processing?

4. Many law enforcement agencies require a "property receipt" or "evidence list" of all evidence collected at a crime scene. What should be included on that list? Be sure to keep in mind science and legal requirements.

CRIME SCENE RECONSTRUCTION

Exercise Q

Final Scene Survey

Learning Objective

- To learn and practice the process of final evaluation of the on-scene crime scene investigation.

The case investigation never technically ends, but there will be a time when the on-scene activities must reach a conclusion. The on-scene activity will bring an end to the evidence recognition and collection. You cannot go back to the scene. Be sure that all pertinent physical evidence has been documented, found, and properly collected. Keep in mind that the collection, packaging, and preservation directly influences the success of the forensic testing to be performed on the evidence; improper collection or packaging means no laboratory results or inadmissibility in court. Communication with all investigators should help with the determination of the scene being released. It is good practice to go back over all the team responsibilities at this point. A "fresh" set of eyes always helps. At this step in the scientific crime scene investigation, a break or getting away from the crime scene will assist with this reflection step. Once all the information has been processed and completed, release the crime scene.

Crime Scene Investigation Laboratory Manual, Second Edition
http://dx.doi.org/10.1016/B978-0-12-812845-9.00017-0

LABORATORY EXERCISE

This exercise will illustrate the process used as part of the final scene survey.

Laboratory Data Sheet

You are given the same crime scene from Exercise F: a homicide investigation in a bedroom (see Fig. Q.1).

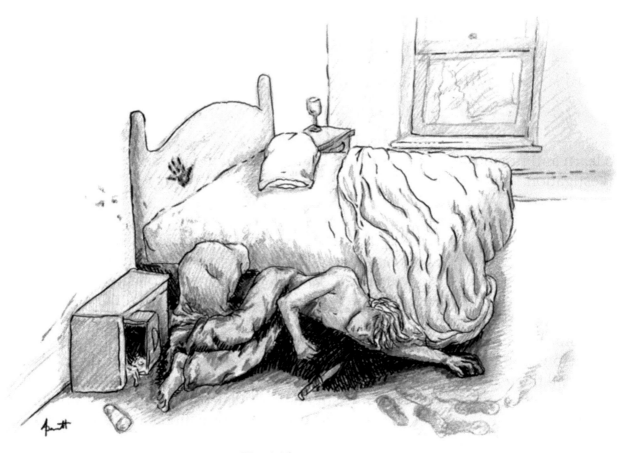

FIGURE Q.1   Homicide scene. *Courtesy of Allyson Parrott.*

Answer the following questions as an illustration about a final scene survey for this specific scene:

1. Did you collect the bedsheets? How? If you did not collect them, why not?

2. Was the bed moved? Was the area under the bed photographed after it was moved? Why or why not?

3. Was the area underneath the victim documented and searched? Why or why not?

4. Who did you use to accompany you for the final scene survey? Why?

DISCUSSION QUESTIONS

1. What happens after the final scene survey?

2. If new evidence is found during the final scene survey, what should a crime scene investigator do?

Exercise R

Crime Scene Reconstruction: Wound Dynamics

Learning Objective

- To identify different types of wounds to determine how they were created.

CRIME SCENE RECONSTRUCTION

Crime scene reconstruction is the process of determining or eliminating the events and actions that occurred at the crime scene through analysis of any crime scene patterns, the location and position of the physical evidence found at the crime scene, and the laboratory examination of the physical evidence. Crime scene reconstruction involves not only scientific scene analysis, interpretation of the scene pattern evidence, and laboratory examination of physical evidence but also an individual's life experiences, reasoning or simple logic, and even common sense.

It is often important to determine the actual activities of a crime by limiting the possibilities that resulted in the crime scene or the physical evidence as encountered. The possible need to reconstruct the crime is one major reason for maintaining the integrity of a crime scene. It should be understood that reconstruction is different from "reenactment," "recreation," or "criminal profiling." Reenactment in general refers to having the victim, suspect, witness, or another individual reenact the event that produced the crime scene or the physical evidence based on their knowledge of the crime. Recreation is to replace the necessary items or actions back at a crime scene through original scene documentation. Criminal profiling is a process based upon the psychological and statistical analysis of the crime scene, which is used to determine the general characteristics of the most likely suspect for the crime. Each of these types of analysis may be helpful for certain aspects of a criminal investigation.

Crime Scene Investigation Laboratory Manual, Second Edition
http://dx.doi.org/10.1016/B978-0-12-812845-9.00018-2

However, these types of analysis are rarely useful in the solution of a crime. Crime scene reconstruction is based on the ability to make observations at the scene, the scientific ability to examine physical evidence, and the use of logical approaches to theory formulations.

Crime scene reconstruction is based on scientific experimentation and on past personal and professional experiences. It involves consideration and incorporation of all investigative information, with physical evidence analysis and interpretation molded into a reasonable explanation of the crime and its related events. Logic, careful observation, and considerable experience, both in crime scene investigation and forensic examination of physical evidence, are necessary for proper interpretation, analysis, and, ultimately, crime scene reconstruction. Crime scene reconstruction is a process that uses "the present," the crime scene and its evidence, to reach conclusions about "the past," how the crime scene came to be.

WOUND DYNAMICS

Wounds and wound causes are the responsibility of the forensic pathologist or medical examiner as part of a criminal investigation. The crime scene reconstructionist will work with the medical examiner to use the type of wound to help determine the activities that caused the wounds found on the body. Many wounds are distinctive and therefore indicate a specific wounding mechanism and type of instrument or weapon used. It is possible for wounds to exhibit more than one character, but with experience, the reconstructionist can identify wound types and mechanisms of cause. The broad categories of wound types are firearm, sharp force, blunt force, asphyxia, burns/chemical, poisoning, explosion, and electrical. See Chart R.1 for a summary of wounds and characteristic appearances.

CHART R.1   Chart of Wound Types

Type of Injury	Characteristics	Other Information
Firearms	Entry, exit, grazing, penetrating, perforating, lacerating	Gases, soot, wadding, gunshot residue
Sharp force	Incised (cuts), stabbings (punctures), combination	Chops—sharp and blunt force; heavy weapons
Blunt force	Crushing, abrasions (scraping), contusion (bruising), lacerations (tearing), fractures (bones breaking)	May appear as cuts
Asphyxia	Strangulations—ligatures, manual, hanging, smothering, suffocation, postural, chest compression chemical Drowning—submersion, immersion, hypothermal	
Burns/chemical	Hypothermal—lack of heat Hyperthermal—too much heat Burns—fire and chemical	Temperature extremes
Poisons	Special toxiocology Acute (rapid) Chronic (over period of time)	Allergic reactions too
Explosions	Flying debris, secondary fires (burns), blast compression	
Electrical	Cardiac-ventricular fibrillation, asystole (heart stops) Respiratory Muscle contractions Heat (see above)	

LABORATORY EXERCISE

For this exercise, use Chart R.1 to identify the type of injury or wound that is shown. This identification of wound type will allow for determination of how the wound was made.

Laboratory Data Sheet

The following images present wound dynamics. Identify the type of wound and the activity that caused the wound.

Wound #1:

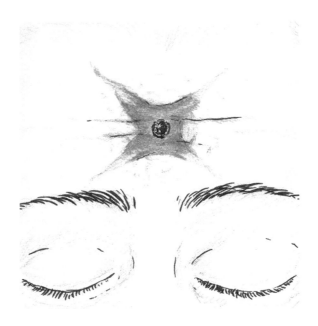

Wound #2:

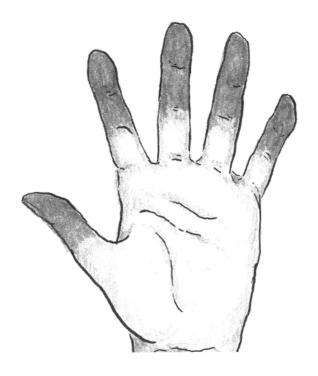

Wound #3:

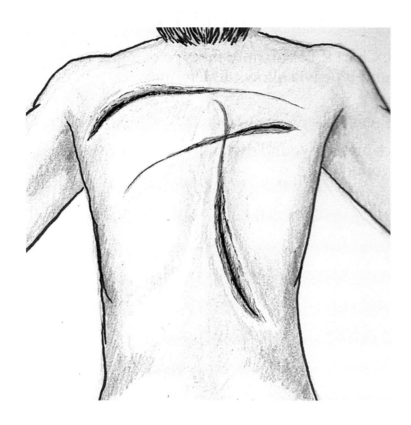

Wound #4:

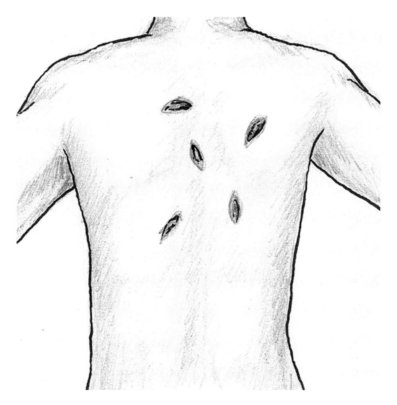

DISCUSSION QUESTIONS

1. Who is the official responsible for wound dynamic identification? Can an experienced crime scene investigator identify wound dynamics? If so, how would this be useful?

2. The identification of wound type and cause may or may not be part of the autopsy. What must a crime scene reconstructionist do to obtain this information?

Exercise S

Crime Scene Reconstruction—Glass Fracture Patterns

Learning Objective

- To utilize glass fracture patterns as a means for the determination of the sequence of glass fracturing and an identification of the origin of force that caused the facture.

Broken glass at crime scenes can sometimes aid in reconstruction and provide information about the events that took place. Glass fracture patterns can be present at a wide variety of crime scenes including burglary, criminal mischief, shooting incidents, and fire scenes. For this exercise the reconstruction information that can be obtained by studying glass fracture patterns includes the following:

- Direction of impact force applied (from inside out or outside in)
- Determination of the sequence of firing, direction of firing, and the type of firearm for the projectile holes present

The use of glass fracture patterns in crime scene reconstruction relies on careful recognition, documentation, and examination of radial, stress, and concentric glass fracture markings such as rib marks.

To conduct even a basic reconstruction based on glass fracture evidence, investigators should be familiar with the different categories of glass and how each type of glass generally fractures. Glass is an amorphous, supercooled liquid, composed primarily of silicon dioxide (sand). There are three general classes of glass: plate (window glass), tempered, and safety. Each class has certain characteristics and will fracture differently.

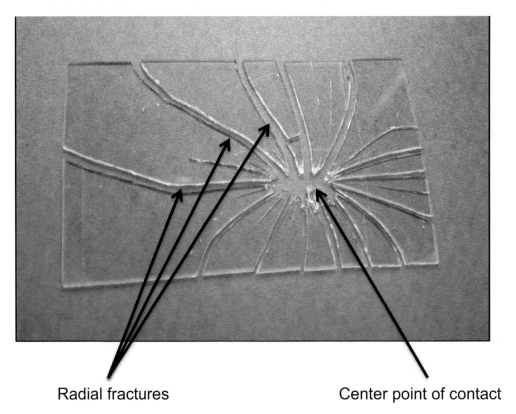

Radial fractures   Center point of contact

FIGURE S.1   Plate glass window fractures.

Plate glass is a common variety of glass used to make windows and mirrors. When plate glass is exposed to a force significant enough to break the surface tension and thus the glass, characteristic pie-shaped glass shards are formed. If broken glass remains in the frame, the observed fracture pattern will consist of a center point where the force contacted the windowpane, with radiating (radial) fracture lines going out from the center point (see Fig. S.1).

Fig. S.2 shows the edge of a radial glass fracture. By examining the broken edge of a piece of glass along a radial line, you can determine the direction of force. This analysis is helpful in determining from which side of the glass the force was applied that caused the window to be broken.

Fig. S.3 shows the progression of force being applied to a plane of glass, causing radial cracks to be formed with rib marks. The rib marks will reflect the side to which the force was applied.

Safety glass is found in automobile windshields. Safety glass is two separate panes of plate glass adhered together with a clear laminated layer between the glass panes. Although this glass fractures in a similar way to plate glass, it remains intact after breaking due to the laminate layer. Safety glass was designed to reduce injuries to passengers should

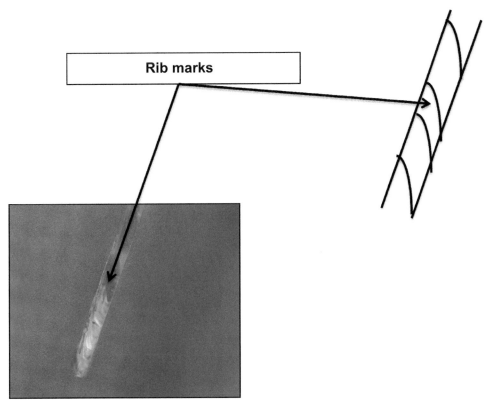

FIGURE S.2   Rib marks on a radial fracture surface.

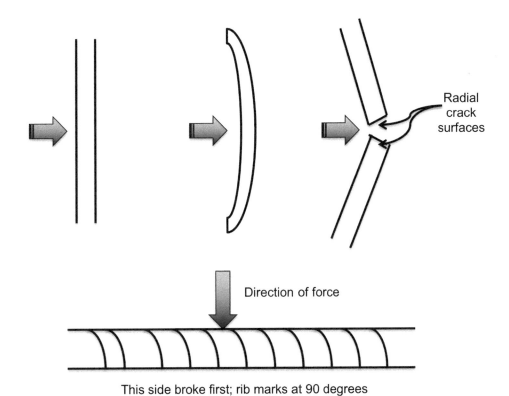

FIGURE S.3   Determination of the direction of force based on radial cracks.

they have an accident. Caution must be exercised when interpreting safety glass fracture patterns because there are two separate panes of glass that will have independent radial fractures.

Because safety glass remains intact, it can provide valuable information in reconstruction of shooting incidents. The direction of each gunshot can be determined by locating the crater, which is located on the side of glass opposite the impacting force. Also, if more than one bullet penetrates the windshield, it is possible to sequence the shots if the bullet holes are close enough together and their separate radial fracture lines converge. The subsequent bullet hole can be determined because radial lines from that bullet hole terminate where they meet the existing radial line from the prior fracture (see Fig. S.4).

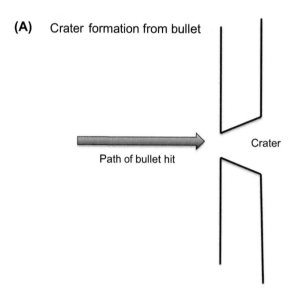

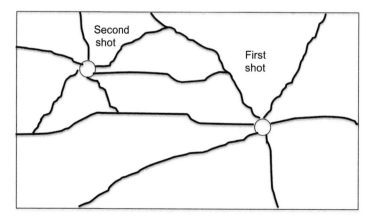

FIGURE S.4   Glass fractures in shooting events.

Tempered glass, used for side windows in automobiles, is a single-pane glass that is durable and difficult to fracture due to its significant surface tension. When enough force is applied to break this surface tension, the entire pane of glass fractures into thousands of small pieces, commonly referred to as dicing. When fractured, the glass dices fall from the window frame into the car and onto the ground. Although it is a daunting task to reassemble the thousands of diced glass fragments, this precise exercise can yield valuable information. It is possible to reassemble the diced window of a shooting and determine the location at which the projectile struck the window, the direction of the projectile flight, an approximate angle of incident, and, in some cases, whether more than one projectile struck the window. This type of reconstruction is very helpful in shooting reconstruction cases in which one or more side windows have been broken by bullets (see Fig. S.5).

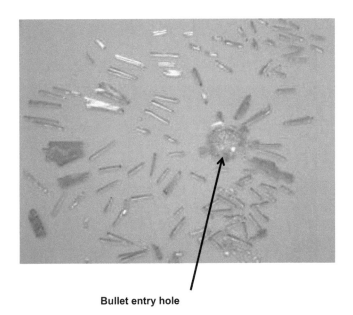

Bullet entry hole

FIGURE S.5   Tempered glass fracture fragments.

LABORATORY EXERCISE

For this exercise the user is presented with a variety of glass fracture patterns. From the patterns, it will be possible to determine the side from which the breaking force was applied in one part of the exercise. For the second part the user will identify the order or sequence of glass fracturing that occurred.

Laboratory Data Sheet

Part One: Using Radial Cracks to Determine Direction of Force

Mark the direction of force using an arrow on the following images:

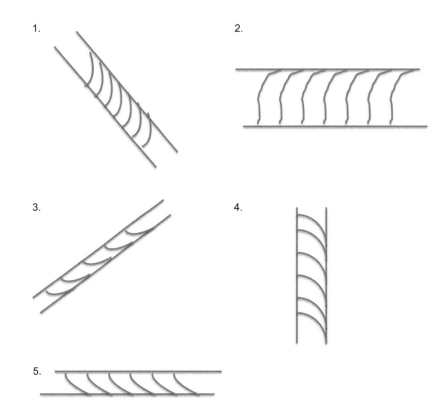

Part Two: Using Radial Cracks to Determine the Order of Firing

Reconstruct the following plate glass windows that were shot, and write in each box the words to describe the order of fire as shown:

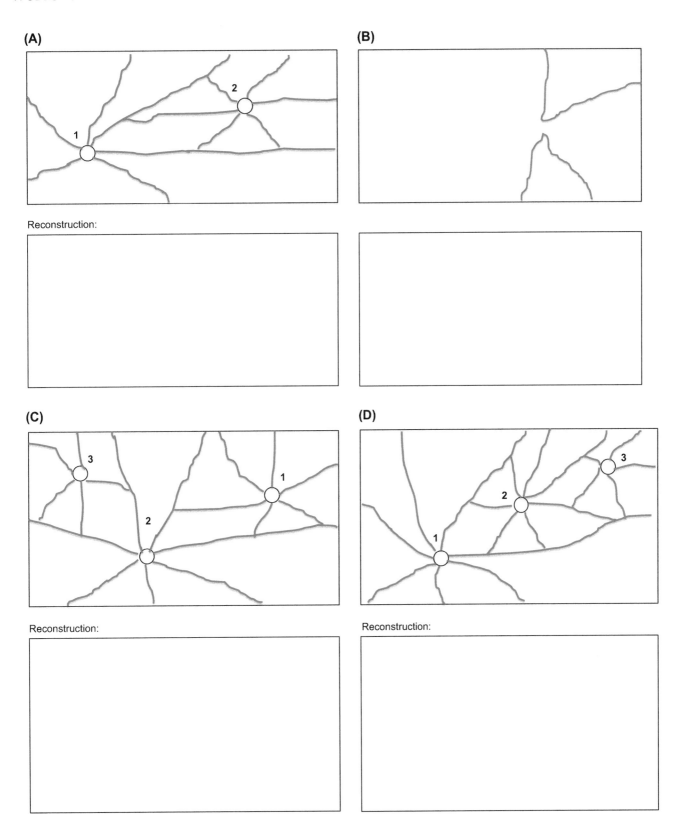

(A)

Reconstruction:

(B)

(C)

Reconstruction:

(D)

Reconstruction:

DISCUSSION QUESTIONS

1. If all the pieces of a broken window have fallen from the frame and lay on the ground or the floor below the window, is it possible to determine the side from which the force to break the window was applied? What must be done?

2. If a bullet hole in a window is circular, what is the angle at which a bullet hit the window? If the bullet hole is oval shaped, what does that mean about the angle at which the bullet hit the window?

Exercise T

Crime Scene Reconstruction: Bloodstain Patterns I

Learning Objectives

- To understand the use of bloodstains' size, shape, and distribution patterns to determine how blood shed occurred.
- To understand how a drop of blood falls and contacts a surface as it affects the shape of the stain.
- To apply the concept of terminal velocity to falling drops of blood.
- To define the directionality of fallen bloodstains.
- To define and use transfer bloodstains for reconstruction purposes.
- To define and apply the mechanisms of blood drops in horizontal motion.
- To begin to utilize bloodstains found at crime scenes to reconstruct bloodshed events.

Bloodstain pattern analysis seeks to define the facts surrounding an investigation by the use of the physical nature of bloodstains. Bloodstain pattern analysis is the use of the size, shape, and distribution patterns of the bloodstains found at a crime scene to reconstruct

Crime Scene Investigation Laboratory Manual, Second Edition
http://dx.doi.org/10.1016/B978-0-12-812845-9.00020-0

the bloodshed event(s). Bloodstain patterns reveal not "who" but "what" with regard to the circumstances of bloodshed. The information imparted by blood patterns for reconstruction purposes include the following:

- Type of blood droplets
- Direction of travel of the blood droplets
- Distance of blood source to target surface
- Angle of impact of blood droplet
- Determination of blood trails, their direction, and the relative speed of their horizontal motion
- Nature of the force used to cause the bloodshed
- Nature of the object used to cause bloodshed, the number of blows involved, and relative location of persons/objects near bloodshed
- Sequencing of multiple events associated with the bloodshed
- Interpretation of transfer or transfer patterns

BASIC BLOODSTAIN PATTERNS

Blood is a fluid mixture of cells, proteins, and ions suspended in a serum, which affect its fluid dynamics. As such, the environment affects blood, a non-Newtonian fluid, but it does not break up in flight and will deposit as a single stain. If the drop breaks into smaller drops, it is because some outside force has been added. Bloodstain patterns found at crime scenes will fall into three broad categories: passive bloodstain patterns, spatter patterns, and special bloodstain configuration patterns. See Fig. T.1.

Each category of pattern will be briefly examined to provide basic information about bloodstain patterns for reconstruction purposes. Additional reading, careful study, controlled experiments, and significant practice must be undertaken for proper bloodstain pattern analysis.

PASSIVE BLOODSTAIN PATTERNS

The fluid dynamics of dropping blood are responsible for the patterns produced. The surface tension of the liquid blood causes the blood drops produced from a blood source to be spherically shaped. The blood drops have a viscosity four times that of water, and when released from the blood source they will oscillate slightly during free fall. Blood possesses an adhesive quality that provides for a small amount of it to adhere to most surfaces.

Passive

    Transfer-swipe,wipe

    Drops-single,multi,trail

    Flow

    Large Volume-saturation,

      free flow, pooling

Spatter

    Impact-gunshot,blunt force,

      sharp force,pools

    Secondary Mechanism-

      2° spatter

    Projected-castoff, arterial,

      expirated

Special Patterns

    Clotted

    Diluted

    Diffused

    Insects

    Sequenced

    Voids

FIGURE T.1   Bloodstain pattern categories.

Many factors will influence the size and shape of the bloodstain once the drop reaches a target surface. A free-falling drop of blood will generally produce circular-shaped patterns when impacting a surface. If the distance a drop of blood falls is increased, it produces a circular pattern showing an increase in the stain's diameter until the terminal velocity of the drop is reached. At this height and above, the diameter of the resulting circular stain will remain constant. It is for this reason that a reconstruction of a drop of blood's **distance fallen** can be done by examination of a bloodstain's diameter. See Fig. T.2.

The target **surface texture** for dropping blood can also affect the size and shape of the bloodstain pattern. Hard, nonporous surfaces will produce circular stain patterns that have smooth edges, whereas softer, porous surfaces will produce spatter stains that are scalloped or have rough edges. See Fig. T.3.

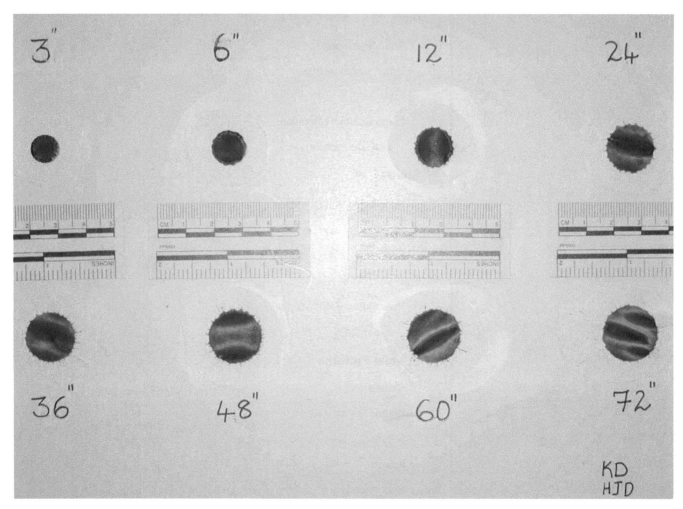

FIGURE T.2   Diameter of bloodstain versus distance fallen.

The above stains fell 12 inches.

FIGURE T.3   Surface texture effects.

V. CRIME SCENE RECONSTRUCTION

DIRECTIONALITY: DIRECTION OF TRAVEL AND ANGLE OF IMPACT

The shape of the resulting bloodstain is changed when the angle at which a blood drop impacts a surface is changed. As the angle of impact is made smaller or more acute, the bloodstain pattern will become more oval, elongated, or elliptical in shape. The impact direction of a drop of blood can also be determined. The "tail" of the blood-stain generally points to the direction of travel of the blood drop. In turn, the blood origin of a drop can be determined. This direction of travel and the angle of impact are referred to as the **directionality** of a bloodstain pattern. The **angle of impact** can be determined from measurements of the length (the extra tail of the bloodstain repre-sents additional force or a bounce effect and is not part of the original drop of blood) and the width of the bloodstain. The trigonometric relationship between the ratio of the long axis (length) versus the short axis (width) of a bloodstain can be measured. See Fig. T.4.

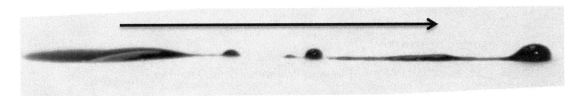

Direction of Travel

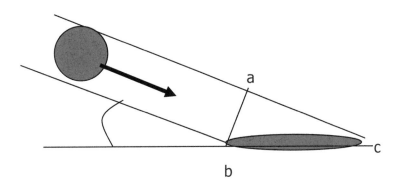

arcsin i = distance ab/distance bc

FIGURE T.4   Directionality: direction of travel and angle of impact.

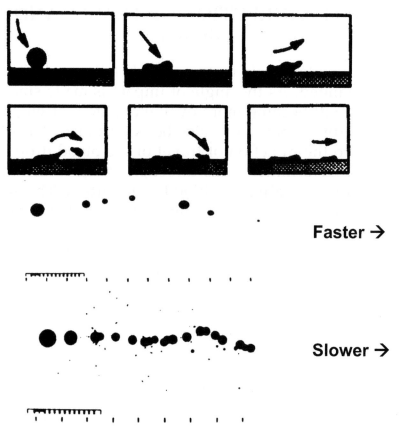

Faster →

Slower →

FIGURE T.5   Blood trails and horizontal motion.

BLOOD TRAILS OR BLOOD IN HORIZONTAL MOTION

Blood trails are frequently found at crime scenes. Careful examination and analysis of the trail pattern will provide information about the direction of travel and the relative traveling speed of the blood source. As the speed of travel of the blood source in a horizontal motion is increased, more elongated shapes of the individual stains will result, and the distance between bloodstains will be increased in the blood trail. See Fig. T.5.

TRANSFER BLOODSTAIN PATTERNS

Transfer bloodstain patterns occur when blood adhering to an object or body is transferred onto a new location or surface. The resulting transfer pattern retains the shape of the original bloody object due to a stationary or static transfer. Therefore, the original bloody object can be identified, and a reconstruction of activity at the crime scene is accomplished. For example, a bloody fork that is placed on a bed sheet will leave a transfer–transfer pattern in the shape of the fork (see Fig. T.6).

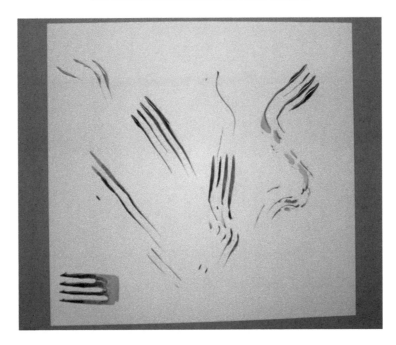

FIGURE T.6   Transfer pattern.

Transfer patterns can be formed due to folded bloody surfaces. Two similar bloody imprints may result from the same object, or one image may result from the other bloody image, hence creating a "butterfly" or mirror image of the original stain (see Fig. T.7).

Transfer patterns can often be created though dynamic motions. When an unstained object moves through a bloody surface or an existing bloodstain, the resulting pattern is called a **wipe pattern**. Examination of the wipe can often show the motion of the original unstained object. A wipe pattern is also produced when a moving bloody object transfers an unstained surface. See Fig. T.8.

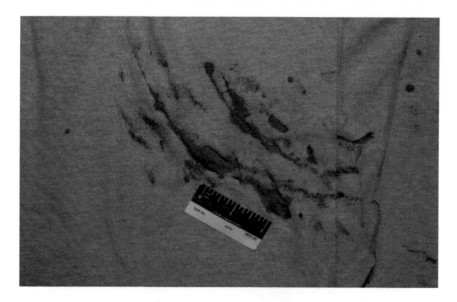

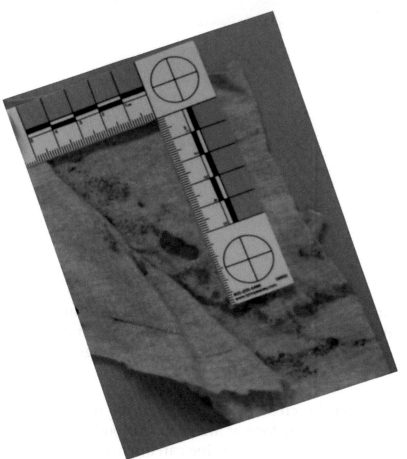

FIGURE T.7   Transfer pattern due to folded surfaces.

FIGURE T.8   Transfer pattern with motion.

LABORATORY EXERCISE

In this exercise the user will begin to understand the patterns produced by falling drops of blood by changing the distance that the blood falls and by changing the surface on which the drops fall. Other parts of the exercise will allow for determination of the blood drops directionality, observe the changes to blood trails based on the speed by which the source is moving, and finally, to use the shapes of bloodstain to identify the original blood object that made a stain.

Laboratory Data Sheet

The size, shape, location, number, and distribution of bloodstains, if examined properly, can allow for determinations of post–bloodshed movement and direction and other reconstruction information. This experiment will allow the student to experiment with the scientific basis and other aspects of bloodstain pattern analysis.

Part One: Stain Diameter Versus Distance to Target and Surface Effects
Procedure
1. Fill the pipette with blood and mount it to a ring stand.
2. Place a target surface beneath the pipette.
3. Using a ruler, set the pipette to a known target distance.
4. Release a single drop of blood, and let it fall onto the target.
5. Repeat using at least five different distances, three less than 48″ and two above 48″. Use three different target surfaces with different textures (paper towel, floor tile, poster board, etc.).
6. When the blood has dried, measure the stain diameter and record the measurements in a data chart.
7. Record observations of the blood spatter's edges for the different textured surfaces.

Part Two: Stain Shape and Impact Angle
Procedure
1. From a constant height, fill a pipette with blood and allow a drop to fall onto a paper target at a 90 degrees angle (be aware that the angle can be measured with respect to either the vertical or the horizontal, but remain constant).
2. Repeat step 1, varying the impact angle (using whole number increments makes this easier).
3. Allow the stains to dry. Accurately measure the length and width of the elliptical stains formed and calculate their width/length ratios (record in data chart).
4. There is a trigonometric relationship between the sine of the angle of impact and the width/length ratio. Calculate the impact angles using the sine function.
5. Prepare a data chart of width/length versus chosen impact angle.
6. Graph this data.

Part Three: More Impact Angle Calculations
Procedure

Given the following bloodstains, select three. Mark the direction of travel of the individual stains, and then calculate the individual angles of impact. Remember significant figures.

Part Four: Blood Trails and Changing Horizontal Motion
Procedure

1. Roll 6–8 ft of butcher paper out onto the floor.
2. Fill a long-nose glass pipette with blood, and then, using your finger over the end, stop the flow.
3. Standing at one end of the paper, release your finger to let the blood drip out of the pipette at a constant rate, and at the same time *walk slowly* to the other end of the paper while holding the dropping distance constant.
4. Mark these bloodstains. *Observe their shapes, sizes, and the distance between stains.*
5. Refill the pipette; repeat the experiment, *walking faster* than the previous walking speed.

6. Refill the pipette again; repeat the experiment, *moving even faster* (almost running).
7. Cut out representative samples of the three different patterns, or use drawings or sketches; label the direction of travel, and discuss any differences in shape between the bloodstains.

Part Five: Transfer Patterns

This part of the exercise will require preparation of some bloody impressions. Common objects can be dipped in blood and placed on the paper target surfaces. Direct transfer and wipe/swiping motions should be used. Allowing the patterns to dry and covering them with clear transfer paper preserves the patterns.

Procedure

1. Examine the various bloodstain impression patterns.
2. Examine the various objects.
3. Correlate at least four patterns with the object that made the pattern.
4. Photograph or make a drawing of the bloodstain impression with the correlated object.

DISCUSSION QUESTIONS

1. What would a graph of the distance falling versus the diameter of a stain look like? How would the absorptive surfaces change the graph versus a nonabsorptive surface such as poster board?

2. Was the graph in Part Two a sine curve? What was missing from your graph to identify the sine curve?

3. Did you include the "tails" of the stain when you measured the length of the stains? Should they be included or excluded? Why?

4. What could be done to more easily obtain the measurement of the widths and lengths of the bloodstains? Why are significant figures important in the calculation of impact angles?

5. Why is it important to keep the source of blood in Part Four steady and not swinging back and forth or moving up and down? What would be the effect of it moving?

6. If you are not able to identify an object that made a transfer bloodstain at a crime scene, what could be done to help the identification? Is this possible in all crime scene investigations?

Exercise U

Crime Scene Reconstruction: Bloodstain Patterns II

Learning Objectives

- To define spatter bloodstain patterns.
- To recognize the appearance of impacted bloodstain patterns and use them to determine where bloodshed occurred.
- To recognize and understand repetitive drip patterns of blood.
- To recognize and understand projected blood patterns.

This laboratory exercise will continue the study of the use of bloodstain patterns for crime reconstruction. The second basic category of bloodstains is "spatter." Spatter bloodstain patterns are made from blood that has additional force or motion given to it, more so than passive drops.

Crime Scene Investigation Laboratory Manual, Second Edition
http://dx.doi.org/10.1016/B978-0-12-812845-9.00021-2

IMPACTED BLOODSTAIN SPATTERS PATTERN

Impact bloodstain patterns are produced when more energy than gravity has been added to the blood source. The force added to the blood causes the blood to break into smaller-sized spatters. The smaller-sized blood sphere spatters are relative to the amount of force or energy involved, both internally and externally. A constant internal force comes from the body's internal blood circulation system. The external force (energy) comes from the force that created the bleeding or the force exerted on the blood source (wound dynamics). The individual blood drop's directionality property remains unchanged; only the resulting bloodstains are smaller when they reach the target surface. See Fig. U.1.

Ahead, we will use this behavior to determine the origin of the impact or where the bloodshed occurred. Generally, impacted blood falls into two types: medium- and high-force impact spatter. See Fig. U.2. Medium-force impact spatter is produced by a force associated with beatings and blunt or sharp force trauma. The size of this spatter is much smaller than that of passive drops. High-force impact spatter is almost always associated with the use of firearms (explosions or high-speed collisions can produce similar patterns). The spatter has a mist-like appearance. It is difficult to see, easily overlooked, and can be altered or lost without careful handling of the physical evidence.

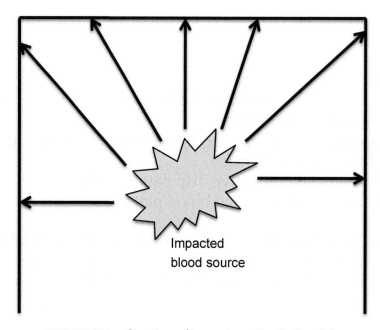

FIGURE U.1   Creation of impact spatter (2-D only).

Medium-force impact spatter.

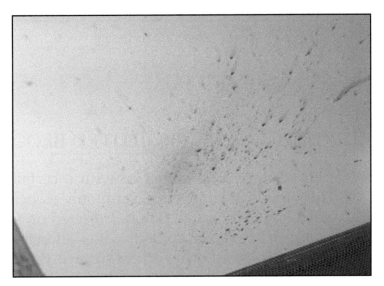

FIGURE U.2   High-force impact spatter.

REPETITIVE DRIPPING PATTERNS

When bloodshed occurs, it is not uncommon for the bleeding source to continue to bleed out. This bleeding will cause blood to drip into an increasing pool of blood, causing secondary spatters to be produced. These secondary spatters bounce and make for smaller stains around the pool of blood. If sufficient blood drips and time passes, a blood pool is created that obliterates the smaller spatter. The repetitive dripping pattern into a pool shows no motion, but with motion it can create a cluster pattern of passive drops. See Fig. U.3.

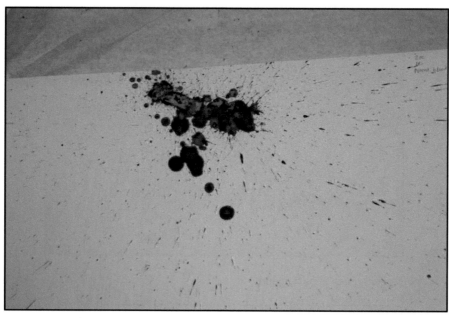

FIGURE U.3   Repetitive dripping.

ARTERIAL GUSHES (PROJECTED BLOOD)

An increased quantity of blood impacting a surface with a certain amount of force is known as *projected blood*. This bloodstain pattern is commonly associated with major injuries with open wounds with a large amount of blood projected on vertical surfaces, such as by arterial gushes. This pattern has sharp, spinous edges and easily shows movement. If the larger quantity of blood is deposited on a vertical surface, the blood will flow downward as it is acted on by gravity and will produce a **flow pattern** of the blood. Arterial gushes deposited on horizontal surfaces show the projection and the increased volume of blood into pools. See Fig. U.4.

FIGURE U.4   Arterial gushes.

AREA OF ORIGIN OF BLOODSHED DETERMINATIONS

As shown previously, when a bloodshed event occurs by external forces or is impacted, the blood will travel out in all directions. It maintains its direction of travel and impact angle. Therefore, when impacted bloodstains are found at a crime scene, after documentation, those bloodstains can be used to determine where the impact occurred by the directionality of the individual stains in the overall pattern.

The **area of origin** of bloodshed is determined by a two-step process. First, a representative sample of individual spatter in the pattern is selected. Each stain's **direction of travel** is marked by placing a line through the center of each stain in the direction of its origin. The lines will converge in an area called the "point of convergence." See Fig. U.5. The second step will use the impact angle of each individual spatter and add a third dimension to the reconstruction. The impact angle of each line is calculated. By using a protractor to "lift" the lines to the correct angles, the lines will form the "area of origin" of the impacted bloodshed event. See Fig. U.6.

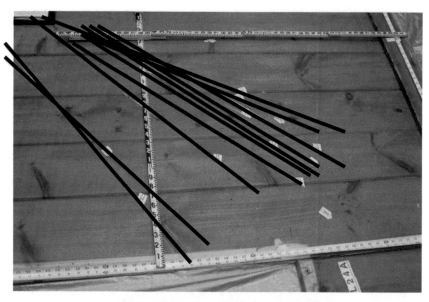

FIGURE U.5   Point of convergence.

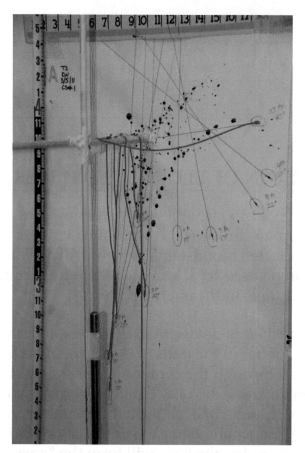

FIGURE U.6   Point of origin of bloodshed.

It is good practice to use more individual spatters than fewer spatters. The area of origin of bloodshed or area of impact determinations will allow the reconstruction of the nature of the force used, the sequence of events, and the relative position of persons or objects near the impacted source.

LABORATORY EXERCISE

For this second set of exercises the user will we given a chance to impact blood and observe the resulting spatter created. Following exercises will allow for the observation of repetitive drip patterns and projected blood patterns. Finally, the user will create some pseudo-impact spatter and using the two-step process describe be able to identify an area of origin of bloodshed from the patterns.

Laboratory Data Sheet

Part One: Impacted Blood Spatter

A closet or small room that can have its walls covered with white butcher paper is the best method for "experiencing" impact spatter. A blood-soaked sponge can be impacted with hands, feet, or any other object of choice. Be sure to wear paper jumpsuits and coverings for hands, feet, and heads. It is an impressive sight to observe the impact spatter, but it is not so impressive to clean up or dispose of the blood-covered walls. An alternate method is to select a medium-sized cardboard box that can be sealed. Cut a 4″ × 4″ opening on one side, and cut the top along three sides for easy opening and closing. Place approximately 1 mL of blood in the center of the box and, while using the 4″ × 4″ opening and a club of choice, impact the blood. The impact spatter should be produced. Record the spatter photographically or by sketching.

Part Two: Repetitive Dripping Blood (and Distance Falling)

Procedure

1. Using a syringe as a holding container with a 6 in length of tubing attached to the end with a closed pinch clamp, add 1 mL of blood.
2. Keep the clamp closed on the rubber tubing to hold the blood in the container.
3. Center the tubing over a paper target by holding it steady.
4. Set the distance falling at a height of 24 in.
5. Quickly open the clamp so as to release all the blood volume and begin the dripping process.
6. Repeat at a distance falling of 72 in.
7. Save and compare the targets from the two heights or draw/sketch the resulting patterns.
8. If time permits, set the 24 in falling distance, and when the dripping begins, slowly move the tubing around to observe the difference in the resulting bloodstain pattern.

Part Three: Projected Blood (and Distance Falling)

Procedure

1. Using a syringe, draw 1 mL or cc of blood into the syringe.
2. Wipe off any excess blood on the outside of the syringe.
3. Quickly project the blood onto the target surface from a height of 24 in.
4. Immediately after the blood has been projected, wipe the tip of the syringe to prevent extraneous blood from falling on the target.
5. Repeat steps 1–3 using a distance projected of 72 in.

6. Compare the targets obtained in this experiment to the targets in the repetitive dripping blood exercise.
7. Repeat steps 1–3, but try moving the syringe. Compare this pattern to the other patterns with a stationary syringe.

Part Four: Area of Origin of Bloodshed

Procedure

1. Obtain an impacted bloodstain pattern. (Dipping a gloved hand into a beaker of blood can create these patterns. Quickly "flick" the fingers from the point of origin onto 24″×48″ of butcher paper. Vary the flicks' location if making multiple samples, and sometimes add more than one flick to a paper.)
2. Observe and identify the directionality of the bloodstain patterns present.
3. Draw a line through the center axis of a representative sample of the bloodstains back toward the source. The lines should converge.
4. Using the techniques of impact angle determination, calculate the impact angles for the blood spatters chosen for the convergence.
5. Once the impact angles have been determined, attach a string to the leading edge of the bloodstain. With a protractor, lift the string to the correct angle and tape it to the ring stand. The point of origin for bloodshed will be visualized. See Fig. U.7.
6. In the space provided below, diagram (to your best ability) the point of origin. Be sure to label on the sketch the distance from the edge of the target paper (any walls) and the height above the target (floor).

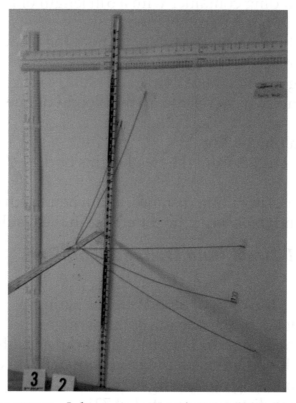

FIGURE U.7   Lab exercise: point of origin of bloodshed.

DISCUSSION QUESTIONS

1. Where will a crime scene investigator find impact spatters while investigating a case in which the suspect was arrested on the scene of an assault and battery? What should be done first?

2. High-force impact spatter, just like GSR, is dependent on caliber and the distance of the barrel to the blood source. Explain this statement.

3. If a projectile passes through the standing victim, high-force impact spatter is propelled forward. Will any spatter be propelled backward? Will it be different in appearance? How so?

4. Could secondary spatters from a dripping wound be confused with impact spatter? Can secondary spatter be masked in any way at a crime scene? Hint: Consider the target surface composition.

5. How does gravity affect impact spatter? Would that change the area of origin determination? If so, how?

Exercise V

Crime Scene Reconstruction: Shooting Investigations

Learning Objectives

- To use gunshot residue (GSR) distribution patterns to determine a range of fire or distance of muzzle to target.
- To use projectile trajectory analysis as a means for determining activities that occurred at the scene of a shooting.
- To understand and use optical methods and physical methods for trajectory determinations.

Reconstruction of shooting scenes is often necessary to determine several factors critical to the investigation. Determining the manner of death—homicide, suicide, or accidental—may be difficult without a reconstruction. A reconstruction can also provide information as to the relative location(s) of the shooter(s) and victim throughout the incident and can help determine the muzzle-to-target distance, which can be a pivotal factor in distinguishing between a homicide and a suicide. Additionally trajectories can be determined so that reconstructions can be performed to provide valuable information about shooter/victim locations, which can in many cases prove or disprove suspect, victim, or witness accounts of shooting scenarios.

Crime Scene Investigation Laboratory Manual, Second Edition
http://dx.doi.org/10.1016/B978-0-12-812845-9.00022-4

The components of a successful shooting investigation include case information from investigating detectives and the crime scene investigation, especially the sketches and location of evidence, autopsy and medical records for wound dynamics, laboratory examination of the physical evidence, and any reconstruction experiments that may have been done. The ability to conduct a meaningful reconstruction in shooting cases is highly dependent on the quality of crime scene documentation, searching, and the collection and preservation of all relevant evidence. In shooting cases, physical evidence such as GSR is prone to being altered or lost if efforts are not made to quickly locate and preserve such evidence.

In summary, shooting investigation reconstructions are based on internal and external ballistics at the crime scene or within the victim's body. GSR patterns are used to determine muzzle-to-target distances and trajectory determinations from entry/exit hole shapes and "straight lines" between them, and bullets and casings are used to determine firearm source by microscopic markings or ejection arcs or distances.

MUZZLE-TO-TARGET DISTANCE DETERMINATIONS

Distance determinations involve a comparison of GSR distribution found on the item collected at the crime scene to controlled, test-fired GSR patterns acquired at various known distances. Each step in the preparation, detection, and comparison of the GSR should be carefully documented. Some of the basic steps in the process are as follows:

- Proper at-scene documentation and handling of evidence
- Visual examination of the target surface—macroscopically and stereomicroscopically
- Enhancement and mapping of distribution of GSR particles by chemical reaction for nitrites or lead (note previous exercise on GSR enhancement)
- Identification and measurement of shotgun pellet patterns if a shotgun was used
- Control tests: particle loss/redistribution control, environmental or condition controls, test target material selection, angle effects, etc.
- Preparation of test targets: proper ammunition use (exact same ammunition and the suspected firearm)
- Objective comparison and evaluation of targets
- Determination of range of firing

Care must be employed in the interpretation of GSR patterns. There are several relevant factors that may affect the resulting pattern. The composition of the target surface will impact the ability of that surface to hold and retain the GSR. Target surfaces that are blood soaked or wet from rain or environmental factors may interfere with the ability to recover GSR or to locate a GSR pattern. Acute angles of incident may also reduce the amount of GSR deposited on the target surface but can be helped by trajectory reconstruction to determine the angle of incident. See Fig. V.1.

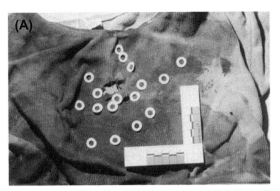

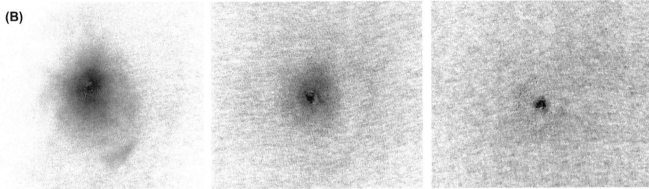

FIGURE V.1   Muzzle-to-target distance determinations. (A) Clothing from victim (*white circles* designate gunshot residue (GSR)). (B) GSR at three distances: 3″, 6″, and 12″.

METHODS FOR TRAJECTORY DETERMINATIONS

The methods for determination of the bullet path or trajectory consist of two types: physical (rods, probes, or strings), or optical (visual sighting or low-power lasers). Whichever method is chosen, careful documentation of the entire reconstruction process should be done by the reconstructionist.

Physical Methods

1. *Entry hole geometry*—The shape of projectile entry and exit holes in target surfaces can be measured, and an estimated angle of entry can be calculated. Most projectile holes are elliptically shaped, and by the use of trigonometry (cosine of the ratio of the width to the length of the hole) the angle of impact can be determined. See Fig. V.2.
2. *Probes and rods*—Probes are useful for establishing projectile trajectories if entry/exit holes are available. Care should be taken not to alter the holes when inserting the probes. It is best to have various sizes or cone collars to help with this process. Probes made of various materials are available. See Fig. V.3.

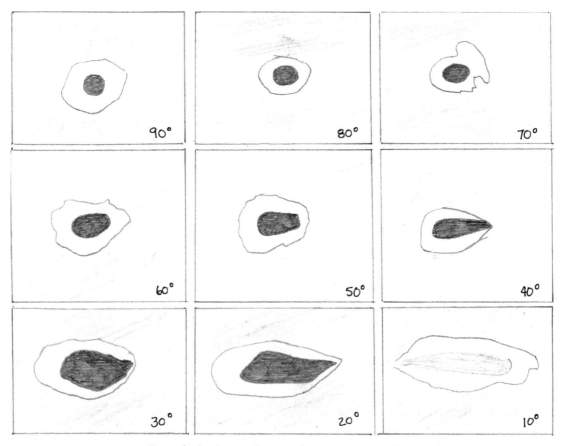

FIGURE V.2   Entry hole shapes (projectiles are entering from right to left).

FIGURE V.3   Physical method of trajectory determination: probes.

V. CRIME SCENE RECONSTRUCTION

FIGURE V.4 Optical method of trajectory determination: red and green lasers. (A) Before documentation. (B) Use of fogging agent for documentation. *Courtesy of Peter Massey.*

V. CRIME SCENE RECONSTRUCTION

3. *Strings*—Longer distances between projectile holes can be aligned using probes with attached strings (sometimes lasers work well here too; see more ahead). Care should be taken not to allow the strings to sag or to be deflected by the sides of the holes, as this would produce significant error.

Optical Methods

1. *Optical sighting*—A simple means of assessing the alignment of projectile holes in reconstruction is to align them visually by looking through them. The alignment achieved is preliminary and lacks precise direction. Photography of the trajectory reconstruction alignment through one projectile hole to the other hole should be attempted.
2. *Low-power lasers*—A laser is useful for aligning projectile holes as it is capable of defining a straight line over a longer distance (see Fig. V.4). Care should be used with long distances because projectile trajectories are influenced by gravity, which can curve the projectile path, especially with lower force projectiles.

EXPERIMENTATION OF TRAJECTORIES

At some crime scenes, when trajectories end within walls, visual access to the termination point must be attained without disturbing the projectile entry hole. Cutting into the wall close to the projectile hole will allow access to this blind projectile hole. Use a probe with the laser attached that is inserted in the projectile hole (carefully avoiding damaging the hole), and the laser is aligned with the probe to effectively "extend" the probe. Hollow probes or fiber-optic probes are good for this process.

Documentation (video and photographic) should be continuous but should at least be done when the laser beam is aligned with two or more projectile holes. Visualization of the laser beam path is enhanced by the addition of mists, smoke, or dust. Inclinometers, protractors, and tape measures can be used to establish the orientation and document the location of the projectile holes in relation to fixed points at the crime scene. After a projectile trajectory has been obtained and documented, a second determination of trajectory should be done.

Substitute intermediate objects or victims of duplicate shape, size, weight, etc. can now be used to "experiment" with reconstruction scenarios without risking damage to the actual evidence. Probes and lasers can be used for these placement experiments (see Fig. V.5).

Postimpact trajectories of projectiles are difficult if the projectile has grazed, ricocheted from, or hit a target with a large angle of impact. For all trajectory reconstructions with intermediate targets, the possibility of **deflection** must be taken into account. In other words, when a projectile passes through an object, there will be some degree of deflection. The degree is established by the nature of the object, its shape, and the manner in which the projectile interacted with it.

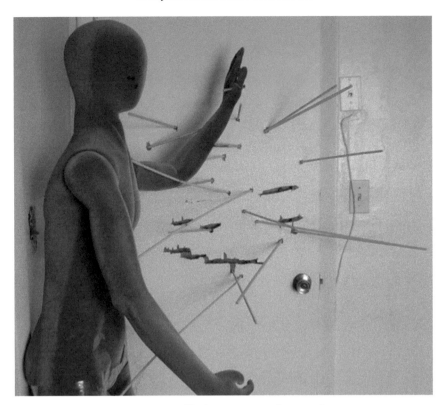

FIGURE V.5   Trajectory experimentation.

PROJECTILES AND CASINGS

Projectiles and casings found at crime scenes can be examined by forensic laboratories to provide valuable information that can be used for reconstruction purposes. The forensic laboratory can provide information about the type of firearms used in the investigation, such as the caliber of the firearm, type of ammunition used, and markings (rifling characteristics such as direction of twist and number or the types of firing pins) on projectiles/casings that may provide a list of possible manufacturers and models. Microscopic examination of the projectile may reveal trace evidence on the projectile, providing information about the types of surfaces contacted by the projectile after firing (intermediate and terminal target materials, silencers, etc.).

Shell casings located at a crime scene can be used for subsequent microscopic comparisons to suspect guns, to determine if they fired that particular cartridge. The location of the shell casings may be useful in determining the approximate location of the shooter in reference to the ejected shell casing. While a majority of semiautomatic or automatic firearms eject to the right, experimentation must be conducted with the actual weapon used or a similar make and model to determine the ejection pattern of that particular gun. When test-firing a weapon to determine the ejection pattern for that gun, several factors must be considered as they may influence the ejection pattern. These factors include the type of ammunition, the shooter's handhold and body position, whether the shooter was stationary or in motion during the ejection, the ground surface that the ejected casings landed on (casings can be easily moved on hard surfaces or stepped on), and environmental factors such as rain and wind. See Fig. V.6.

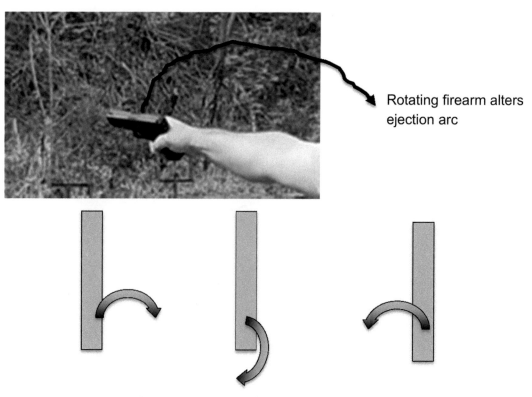

Rotating firearm alters ejection arc

Ejection to the right, back, and to the left

FIGURE V.6   Pistol ejection arc.

LABORATORY EXERCISE

Laboratory Data Sheet

Part One: Range-of-Fire Testing or Muzzle-to-Target Determination

For this exercise, it will be necessary to acquire some known GSR targets. A local shooting range or firearm club may be able to provide them. The best targets are made from old cotton T-shirts or sheets. Squares cut to 18″ × 18″ are a good size for ample collection of GSR. Use at least three different caliber firearms, and marked shooting distances should be contact, in three-inch increments up to 24 in, and then six-inch increments to 36 in. For comparison exercises and blind test studies, be sure to have some duplicate targets shot and designated with letters instead of distance and caliber. It is a good idea to separate each target with a blank piece of paper when stacking the targets for storage.

Assignment: Visually compare the unknown letter target to the known targets, and identify the muzzle-to-target distance for the unknown using the GSR distribution patterns, burn or soot characteristics, and hole diameters. Document the unknown by photography or sketching.

Part Two: Trajectory Determinations or Determinations of Shooter/Victim Locations

For this part of the exercise, it will be necessary to prepare some objects for the trajectory determinations. Hollow walls can be made that will allow for a great amount of variation of trajectory angles and entry/exit holes. Small sections, 18″ × 18″, of walls made with styrofoam insulation material are lightweight and easy to cut and use when creating "bullet holes." The walls may have one or many bullet holes for probing or optic methods of trajectory determination. A commercially available trajectory kit is easy to use, but purchasing wooden dowel rods of diameters consistent with caliber sizes also works. Laser pointers can be used for this exercise as well. Tape measures and protractors will allow the student to reconstruct trajectory determinations accurately.

Assignment: Each student will be given one or more than one shot object or wall for trajectory determination. Depending on the method(s) available (optical lasers or plastic, wood, or metal probes), each trajectory should be determined. Identification of caliber, angle of entry (with respect to the horizontal and the vertical axis), and the location of a possible shooter should be determined. Each trajectory determination should be documented with photography, videography, and sketching.

Part Three: Ejection Pattern of Casings for Determination of Shooter Location

A mock shooting scene will need to be set up with the use of many spent casings. The casings can be bunched together in close proximity as if the shooter and firearm are in one location or can be spaced out as if the firearm and the shooter are ejecting the casings while moving. A little research on the ejection arc for several firearms will be necessary for this exercise.

Assignment: Document the casings and the scene using photography, videography, and sketching to show the location of the casings in the crime scene. Given a representative sample of firearms from which to choose and knowing the ejection arc pattern for each firearm, reconstruct or determine the location of the firearm/shooter for the crime scene.

DISCUSSION QUESTIONS

1. What are potential sources of error for each of the shooting reconstruction exercises presented (range of fire, trajectory, and ejection-pattern determinations)? What can be done to minimize these potential errors?

2. Why is it important to use the same firearm and ammunition in range-of-fire experiments? How many test-fire targets are needed?

3. When is the best time to make a trajectory determination using optical methods?

4. How would a metal detector be essential for shooting reconstruction activities?

Exercise W

Crime Scene Reconstruction: Report Writing and Practice Scenarios

Learning Objectives

- To use report writing skills to prepare a proper crime scene reconstruction report.
- To practice reviewing crime scene investigation materials for the purpose of reconstructing what happened at the scene.

Theoretically, crime scene reconstruction is the use of the crime scene as investigated, with its physical evidence, the results of the laboratory testing of the physical evidence, life experience, and reasoning (common sense). Practically, crime scene reconstruction is the use of crime scene reports, crime scene photographs, crime scene sketches, autopsy reports (injury reports), all forensic laboratory reports, and any sworn statements of victims, suspects, or eyewitnesses. Putting all the relied-upon information into a report follows this format:

- Purpose, scope, or intent of report: good to restate how crime scene reconstruction is defined or used
- List of material reviewed, scenes visited or observed, and any physical evidence examined or viewed
- Charts and tables work well
- Insert and refer to photographs
- Conclusions reached
- Group areas or locations together
- Insert and refer to photographs

Other general guidelines are to have the report peer-reviewed to prevent any Daubert issues, and do not overcommit or too narrowly limit your conclusions and observations. The latter is accomplished by use of careful wording (consistent with, similar to, inconsistent with available data or facts, inconclusive, cannot be determined with the available information, etc.). As with any scientific methodology, keep an open, objective mind.

Crime Scene Investigation Laboratory Manual, Second Edition
http://dx.doi.org/10.1016/B978-0-12-812845-9.00023-6

Finally, the process of information gathering and its use in reconstruction shows the scientific nature of crime scene reconstruction and will allow for its successful use by investigators.

See Fig. W.1 for a sample crime scene reconstruction report.

Date of report

Address of person receiving report

RE: City of Townville Police Department—Acme Shooting Case

Dear Receiving Person:

I examined the following materials in the above-stated investigation:

[In this section, list anything that was reviewed as part of this reconstruction activity.]

- Rough and finished crime scene sketches
- Various materials of Dr. Woo and Inv. Christmas from the Office of the Medical Examiner, including: autopsy report, case reports and notes, property receipts, death certificate, and finger and palm prints
- Firearms' lab report, lab requests for firearms examination, bench notes, and property receipts relating to examinations on XX/XX/XXXX
- Firearms' lab report and property receipts relating to examinations on XX/XX/XXXX
- Gunshot residue (GSR) analysis request and results of the victim on XX/XX/XXXX
- Cocaine analysis request
- GSR analysis request for analysis of gloves
- GSR analysis results on XX/XX/XXXX
- Sworn statement of Officer Smith, XX/XX/XXXX
- Photographs of crime scene, various pieces of physical evidence, and autopsy
- Townville Police Department crime scene video and video by private investigator

[In the next section, state the definition of crime scene reconstruction, how it is done, and the value of reconstruction. Specifically state what you were asked to do for the specific case in question.]

FIGURE W.1 Sample reconstruction report.

On March 11, 20XX, in the presence of you, Assistant United States Attorney ZZZ, Detectives Pat Smart and CM Shake, I examined the crime scene location in Apartment Q, Townville, USA. This letter will serve as a report of findings from my review of the above materials and the crime scene location.

One of the primary uses of physical evidence in a criminal investigation is to substantiate eyewitnesses', victims', and even suspects' statements about the criminal activity. Crime scene reconstruction is the process of determining or eliminating the events and actions that occurred at the crime scene through analysis of the crime scene patterns, the location and position of the physical evidence, and the laboratory examination of the physical evidence. Reconstruction not only involves scientific scene analysis, interpretation of the scene pattern evidence, and laboratory testing, but also involves systematic study of related information and the logical reasoning leading to the reconstruction.

In the above case investigation, I was asked to utilize the physical evidence, the laboratory testing, the autopsy findings, and other case materials to evaluate the officer's statement and to reconstruct the shooting aspects of the case.

Evaluation of Officer QQQQ's statement of XX, XX, and XXXX

[In this section, state the facts or information that were used as part of the reconstruction. Stay objective.]

Officer QQQQ says that he kicked the bedroom door in the apartment. Footwear impressions found on the door and the broken hinges both on the door and still present in the apartment show that the door was closed, was kicked, and was forced open.

Officer QQQQ relates in his statement that the victim "cracked the door open and he fired two rounds." He goes on to state that "I can see his body; like more than half his body....his right side, which at this time is facing me, and with his right hand he stuck the gun out. He fired two rounds. I heard the shots and I saw the muzzle flash." And he says, "...soon as I saw the gun pointing out, I started discharging my MP-5, which I had in a three-round burst, and while I am firing at him I observed a muzzle flash coming from his handgun, and I just continued firing." The physical evidence at the scene, specifically the bullet trajectories in the bedroom door and the autopsy report identifying bullet locations and trajectories in the body of the victim, does not substantiate the statement. If the victim was standing in the location as reported by Officer QQQQ, then the victim's body would have had many more gunshot wounds, and more bloodstain patterns of various types would have been found at the scene. As shown in Photo #1, in order for the victim to extend his arm through the door

FIGURE W.1   Continued.

V. CRIME SCENE RECONSTRUCTION

and discharge a firearm while the SWAT officer is firing his three-burst rounds, the victim would have sustained a large number of gunshot wounds.

Officer QQQQ elaborates on the reason for firing all of his 30 rounds: "The threat was still in front of me. The offender, he was still pointing his gun at me, and I felt fearful of my life, and the lives of my team members." The bullet trajectories in the bedroom door and in the victim's body disprove this statement. The victim could not have been standing in this location with the door cracked open with the result as shown by the physical evidence. See Photo #2.

Crime Scene Shooting Reconstruction

[In this section, state your reconstruction conclusions based on specific tests, photographs, etc. Insert or refer to photographs as part of appendices to the report.]

The location and position of physical evidence at the crime scene, the autopsy report of gunshot wounds, and the physical dimensions of the apartment were used to reconstruct the shooting. The bloodstain patterns found on the wall next to the bedroom door and the stains on the back of the door show that the victim's hand and arm were in a location adjacent to the stains at a height of approximately 61 inches above the floor. The bullet trajectories in the victim's body and through the door are consistent with the victim standing in a location close to the closet door opening, facing in an easterly direction. The bloodstain patterns found in the bedroom and on the door show that the victim was in the noted location with his hand approximately 4–5 inches from the door when he was shot. See Photos #3 and #4.

The bloodstain pattern evidence, the bullet trajectories in the bedroom door, and the autopsy findings show that the victim was not standing in front of an open door when he was shot. Instead, the evidence shows that he was standing behind a door near the bedroom closet when the team members of the Townville Police Department shot him.

Please do not hesitate to contact me should you have any questions with regard to this report or any other matters of my examination of the investigation.

Sincerely yours,

Signature

Your Name
Crime Scene Reconstructionist

Appendix I. Photographs

FIGURE W.1   Continued.

V. CRIME SCENE RECONSTRUCTION

LABORATORY EXERCISE

Laboratory Data Sheet

For this exercise, materials from a crime scene investigation will be provided. The materials will be a series of crime scene photographs, sketches, and reports, autopsy reports (cause of death, wound descriptions, etc.), and results of laboratory testing of items of evidence. The student is asked to review the materials and begin outline the reconstruction report as to "what happened." No formal report is expected at this time. Additionally include in your reconstruction report any evidence that was not tested but should be to assist in the reconstruction.

Part One: Mock Crime Scene #1

Case Synopsis

This is the death investigation of homeowner Susan Oliver. The scene is a detached garage located on the couple's property. Her soon-to-be ex-husband called 911 and readily admitted to cutting the victim. He stated that he defended himself with his pocketknife after the victim stabbed him twice in the upper left thigh with a 6-foot spear. The victim was found on the ground in a pool of blood with incised wounds to her carotid artery and jugular vein. The suspect retrieved keys to a locked office in the garage from the victim's pocket for access to the telephone. The suspect was found in the office, sitting on the floor, when the first responders and EMS arrived.

Crime Scene Sketch

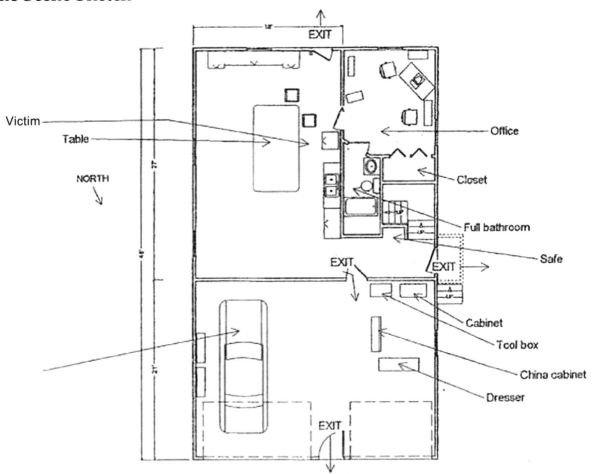

Crime Scene Photos
See Fig. W.2.

FIGURE W.2   Mock Crime Scene #1: selected crime scene photographs.

FIGURE W.2   Continued.

V. CRIME SCENE RECONSTRUCTION

FIGURE W.2   Continued.

FIGURE W.2   Continued.

V. CRIME SCENE RECONSTRUCTION

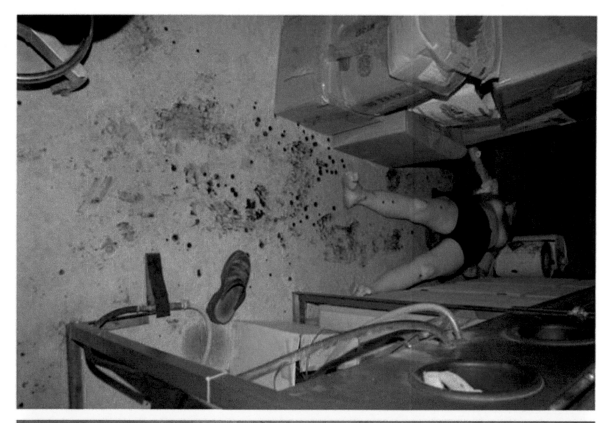

FIGURE W.2   Continued.

FIGURE W.2   Continued.

V. CRIME SCENE RECONSTRUCTION

FIGURE W.2   Continued.

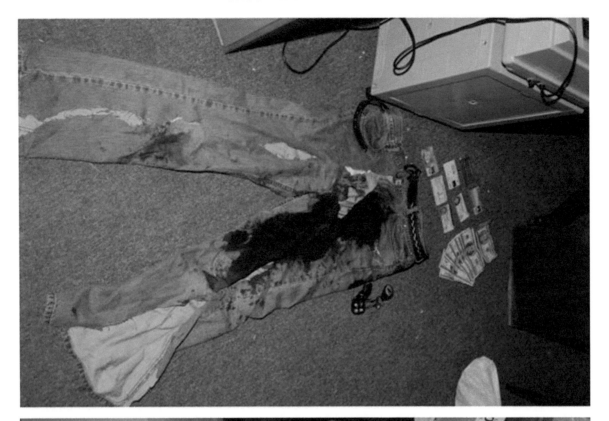

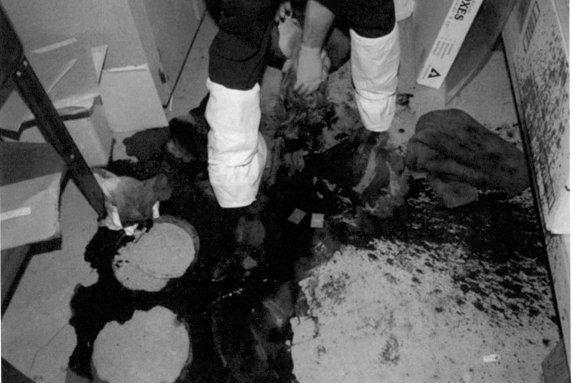

FIGURE W.2   Continued.

V. CRIME SCENE RECONSTRUCTION

FIGURE W.2   Continued.

FIGURE W.2   Continued.

V. CRIME SCENE RECONSTRUCTION

FIGURE W.2   Continued.

FIGURE W.2   Continued.

V. CRIME SCENE RECONSTRUCTION

FIGURE W.2   Continued.

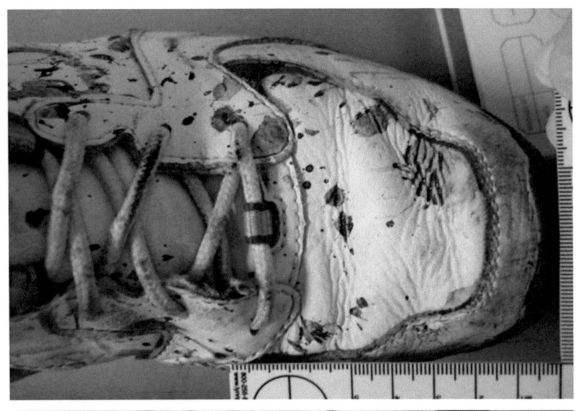

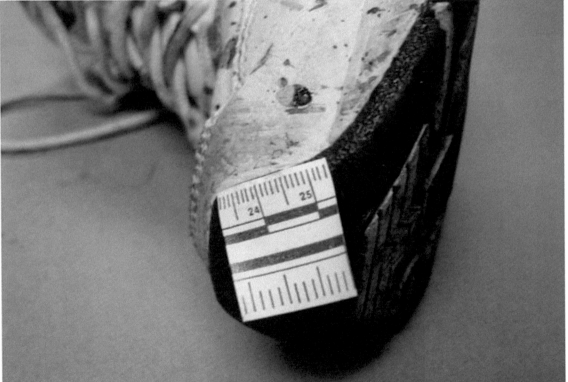

FIGURE W.2   Continued.

V. CRIME SCENE RECONSTRUCTION

FIGURE W.2   Continued.

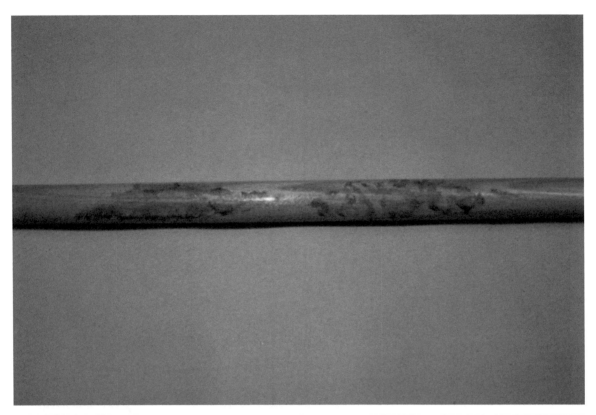

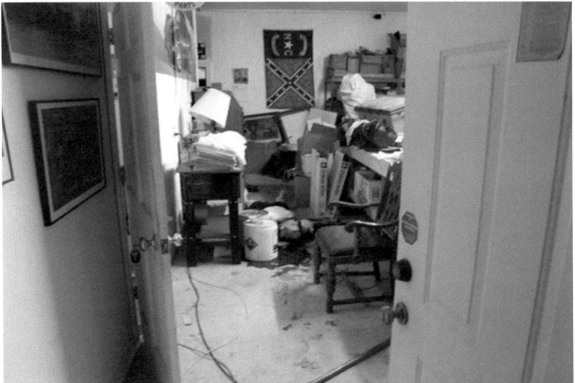

FIGURE W.2   Continued.

V. CRIME SCENE RECONSTRUCTION

FIGURE W.2   Continued.

Autopsy Report

The victim's carotid artery and jugular vein were severed by two incised wounds. The knife wound at the scene is consistent with the weapon used. There are two defensive wounds to the victim's left hand.

Other Hospital Reports

The suspect's wounds were severe in nature, with considerable bleeding. No arteries were damaged. There were two wound paths in the left leg, front to back, with a width consistent with the spear found at the scene.

Forensic Laboratory Testing

Blood Evidence:
- Passive drops in entry way, around the towel pile, near the victim's body, and in the office are consistent with the suspect.
- Arterial gushes on ground are consistent with the victim.
- Bloodstains on the suspect's blue jeans (right pocket, knee, and upper left thigh) are consistent with the suspect.
- Bloodstains on the suspect's T-shirt are consistent with the victim.
- Blood on the spear end is consistent with the suspect; blood impression on the shaft is consistent with the victim. Footwear impression is consistent with the suspect's shoe.
- Blood on the suspect's shoes is a mixture of the victim's and suspect's.

Impression Evidence:
- No latent fingerprints of value were found on the knife or the spear.
- The bloody footwear impressions found at the feet of the victim were a mixture of the victim's and suspect's shoes.
- The bloody footwear impressions found in the entry and pathway to the victim and the office are consistent with the suspect.

No other evidence was tested.

Part Two:—Mock Crime Scene #2

Case Synopsis

This is a homicide by shooting. The victim is a known drug dealer. The suspect is one of his customers. The suspect says that he was defending himself from the victim, who was aggressively pointing a gun at the suspect when the suspect went to the victim's front door to buy some drugs. The victim was shot with two 9-mm rounds retrieved from his body. The suspect was found at his home 5 miles from the crime scene. The victim's wife, who stated that the suspect came up to the door and fired one round into the victim through the screen door, witnessed the shooting. According to the wife, the victim kept his loaded weapon and drug stash in his vehicle parked in the driveway.

Crime Scene Sketch

None was done by the investigators.

Crime Scene Photographs

See Fig. W.3 for selected images.

FIGURE W.3   Mock Crime Scene #2: selected crime scene photographs.

FIGURE W.3   Continued.

V. CRIME SCENE RECONSTRUCTION

FIGURE W.3   Continued.

FIGURE W.3 Continued.

V. CRIME SCENE RECONSTRUCTION

FIGURE W.3   Continued.

FIGURE W.3 Continued.

V. CRIME SCENE RECONSTRUCTION

FIGURE W.3   Continued.

Autopsy Report

The victim died due to two gunshot wounds; both were 9-mm caliber rounds. Round #1 (not in any order) entered the front upper chest and remained in the body. It was front to back and slightly upward. Round #2 was lodged in the rib cage of the victim. It passed through the heart and lungs of the victim, back to front, and significantly upward in direction. The second wound would have been immediately incapacitating. Both wounds would have bled a great deal; as a result, the victim would have lost a large amount of blood.

Forensic Laboratory Testing

Blood Evidence:

All the blood evidence (swabs from the scene, mist bloodstains found on the screen door, and mist bloodstains on the left leg of the suspect's sweatpants) is consistent with the victim.

Firearm Evidence:
- The 9-mm firearm found inside the front door of the scene fired the rounds removed from the victim's body.
- The 9-mm firearm found inside the front door of the scene fired the 9-mm casings found at the scene (found near the door and found near the victim's body).
- No GSR was found on the victim's clothing.

No other evidence was tested.

DISCUSSION QUESTIONS

1. What was easy to do in your report writing?

2. What was most difficult to do in your report writing?

3. For Mock Crime Scene #1 what happened? Which items of evidence support the reconstruction? Which items of evidence seem out of place? Are there any unanswered "evidence creation questions"?

4. For Mock Crime Scene #2 what happened? Which items of evidence support the reconstruction? Which items of evidence seem out of place? Are there any unanswered "evidence creation questions"?

Appendix I

Responses to Laboratory Exercise: Data Sheet Questions/Discussions

Exercise A The data sheet is a chart that will have a variety of responses possible.

Exercise B The data sheet is a chart that will have a variety of responses possible.

Exercise C The data sheet is a listing of evidence that will have a variety of responses possible.

Exercise D
    Question 1 The first responder should check on the welfare of the victim while being careful not to change, alter, or contaminate any items of evidence near the victim's body.
    Question 2 The footwear impressions, the knife, the hand impression, the drinking glass, and the wine glass should minimally be protected, but all evidence should be protected and not disturbed.
    Question 3 Set up crime security by establishing barriers to prevent any other entries into the crime scene.

Exercise E The mock crime scene should show x's at all the intersections surrounding the crime scene, an x at the building point of entry, and two x's on either side of the bottom outside corners of the building. For the interior of the scene, all of the rooms beside the main target crime scene with the body, there should be an x in the center of the rooms and the hallway. For the target scene, there should be an x in the center, at the victim for the victim's point of view, at the point of entry, and at the center of each of the four walls (compass points).

Exercise F The responses to the questions will vary as they relate to the crime scene in the figure.

Exercise G The responses to the questions will vary as they relate to the crime scenes in the figures. It is okay to respond to some of the blanks with unknown or make-up responses as long as the evidence is shown in the pictures.

Exercise H See Exercise E for placement of "x's" on aerial view. The placard should be completed with appropriate information. The third part is dependent on the mock scene drawing.

Exercise I

Part Four-A As the aperture was closed down or made smaller with a larger f/stop number, then more of the items in the glass would have been in focus.

Part Four-B As the shutter speed increased the resulting photo would have gotten darker or underexposed. Sometimes it is easier to view the photographs once download onto a computer to observe the photo differences.

Exercise J No lab questions to answer.

Exercise K No lab questions to answer.

Exercise L No lab questions to answer.

Exercise M Enhancement Reagents

Part A False positive reactions with luminol will be seen with a penny, bleach, rust, and some vegetable peroxidases.

Part B The faint blood pattern on the paper may be slow to develop. Try adding heat from a hair dryer or allow the paper to sit over night.

Biological Field Tests

Part B Interference from white or bleached backgrounds will be shown with the use of the UV light. The diluted semen stains will be visible with the UV light up to the 1:2500 dilution.

Exercise N No lab questions to answer. The sections for this lab are easy to observe. Care should be taken as strong acids are used. Eye wear is a good idea.

Exercise O No lab questions to answer.

Exercise P Each of the scenarios will present problem-solving scenarios where the user will have to identify the type of evidence, any searching techniques (physical patterns and the use of alternate light source (ALS) most of the scenarios), any visualization techniques (see previous exercises), and packaging/collections (remember general guidelines).

Exercise Q

Question 1 Yes, wrap the bedsheets into a butcher paper druggist fold and put in a large paper bag. Or No, the bedsheets were not collected because they were search at the crime scene using an ALS with negative results.

Question 2 The bed should have been moved after documentation to search for any evidence that may be under it.

Question 3 As with the bed, the area under the victim must be searched for any evidence that may be present.

Question 4 For real crime scenes, the case detective, if available, is a good person to accompany the lead crime scene investigator for the final scene survey.

Exercise R The wounds are as follows:

#1 = Close range gunshot;

#2 = Burns; chemical or extreme temperature;

#3 = Incised cuts; and

#4 = Stab wounds with double edges.

Exercise S

Part One The direction of the force that caused the facture:

1. Right upper side, downward.

2. Straight down.

3. Lower right side, upward.

4. From right to left.

5. Straight up.

Part Two The reconstruction for the order of fire:

a. Shot #1 followed by shot #2.

b. It is not possible to determine how the window was broken (look for GSR or rib marks).

c. Shot #2 was first followed by shots #1 and #3.

d. The order of fire was #1 followed by #2 followed by #3.

Exercise T

Part One The stains' diameters should increase with increasing distance up to about four feet. The more textured and absorptive surfaces will show lots of edge destruction or no diameter increases.

Part Two The resulting graph should be one-quarter of a sine curve.

Part Four The stains will be almost round and close together for slow walk. As the speed increases the distance between the stains increases and they become more oval shaped with small tails.

Exercise U

Part One The walls, floor, and the top of room (box) should show elongated, small stains and an obvious impact site.

Part Two The repetitive drips show lots of secondary spatters that are mostly round or slightly oval. Diameters are 2–5 mm.

Part Three The projected blood pattern shows very spiney-like spatters with very forceful appearance in center.

Exercise V No lab questions to answer.

Exercise W The lab directions are to write reconstruction reports using the appropriate outline as suggested in the lab.

Appendix II

Exercise Discussion Question Answers

Exercise A

Question 1 No insufficient information or no clear images of all the evidence shown in the photograph (large bloodstain pool in lower right, black object next to wall, etc.).

Question 2 Not all definitions will be applicable but the use of the appropriate definitions assists the investigator to be prepared but not close-minded.

Exercise B

Question 1 Probably, chemical evidence can ordinate from a natural source and conversely, biological evidence is frequently identified by chemicals present in the evidence. The categories help the crime scene investigator better search for, find and collect the evidence.

Question 2 Yes and no. The crime scene investigator assists the detectives by providing information from the evidence only!

Question 3 It is accomplished at the crime scene. Portable instrumentation, such as fingerprint scanners, can be used to positively identify evidence (also FTIR, Raman Spec, DNA analyzers).

Exercise C

Question 1 There are many examples of evidence that corroborative, associative, or individualizable.

Question 2 Advantages: more classification cross-overs allow for a more effective use of the evidence by the investigators.

Disadvantages: more classification cross-overs can also confuse or produce to many nonsubstantive leads for investigators.

Exercise D

Question 1 No. Small changes by the first responder such as opening a door or turning on a light are considered alterations. The crime scene investigator anticipates and accounts for these alterations by communicating with the first responder.

Question 2 Immediately, to preserve any memory of the activities.

Exercise E

Question 1 At the top of each page of the security log there should be a consistent block of information: Case number, date(s)/time on scene, and page number. The log should have the following columns: Name/Agency/Reason on Scene/Date/Time On/Time Out.

Question 2 When the scene is released by the lead detective or lead crime scene investigator.

Exercise F

Question 1 This report will reflect the activities of the preliminary scene survey and will be specific for the scene chosen.

Question 2 They saw the original condition of the crime scene, and they can alert the crime scene investigator to any changes they or others caused at the scene on arrival.

Exercise G

Question 1 This report will reflect the activities of the note taker at the crime scene and will be specific for the scenes documented.

Question 2 No, all known information is essential for establishing the reliability/validity of the crime scene. Of course, any changes or alterations must be recorded.

Exercise H

Question 1 Satellite imagery may be used to supplement note, photographs and sketches.

Question 2 Select three digital camcorders by an Internet search. Responses may vary but features to examine are internal stabilizers, light sensitivity, resolution capabilities, type of image card used, focal length options or zooming ability, battery use and life, etc.

Exercise I

Question 1 Examination quality photograph. Add oblique lighting, scales, documentation within the photograph, and use a tripod.

Question 2 A variety of equipment is commercial available: a variety of light sources (internal or external flashes, alternate light source (ALS)), tripods, ladders, tape measurers, scales, etc.

Question 3 Shutter speed and aperture. Part 4 A. and B.

Exercise J

Question 1 Title, scale used, date(s)-initial on scene and when drawn, names of sketcher and any helpers, compass direction designation, and a legend for evidence identified and abbreviations used.

Question 2 Yes, its exact location must be sketch and measured, but it will have been photographed by examination quality techniques, too.

Question 3 Various answers possible. Be sure to justify response.

Exercise K

Question 1 Yes, a single crime scene could be searched using all geometric patterns. In reality, however, a crime scene investigator would never do all of them to be time efficient and reduce possibility of contaminated evidence already found.

Question 2 The searchers my use lighting aides or enhancement reagents while they search. The searchers should never move or touch the items found.

Exercise L

Question 1 Yes, any item of evidence can be laid out on the bench top in a darkened room and searched with the use of the ALS.

Question 2 Various.
Question 3 Complete darkness helps but the attempts to search with ALS with all amounts of light should be tried first.

Exercise M
Question 1 Some difficulties would include pattern fading before photos are taken, overspraying to wash away the stain, not able to attain a dark room, and false positives. To overcome the above try a different visualization and enhancement reagent not requiring darkness or does not fade like amido black.
Question 2 Stains on immoveable surfaces.
Question 3 The field tests react with stains that are very trace or dilute.
Question 4 No, the positive enhancement color includes blood as being possibly present, there fore, not additional testing is required and the sample should be collect for subsequent laboratory testing where they may run both tests for identification processes.
Question 5 Artichokes, radishes, horseradish, metals-rust, iron, or any substance that behaves as a peroxidase.

Exercise N
Question 1 The positive result means that those substances may be present and that the evidence should be collected and packaged for forensic laboratory testing.
Question 2 The negative result means that those substances are not present (or have be lost, consumed, or alters). The crime scene investigator needs to keep searching the scene.
Question 3 Test the reagent with knowns before ever going to the crime scene.
Question 4 GSR is composed of many of the same chemicals used as explosives.

Exercise O
Question 1 A variety are available.
Question 2 The paper or porous surface may allow for the colored product to be further dispersed or to evaporate away such as ninhydrin in volatile organic solvent, acetone.
Question 3 The penny provides a false positive control. False positives may occur if there is contamination at the scene with nonblood (heme groups) peroxidases such as vegetable or fruit peroxidases.
Question 4 Advantages: sensitive, good contrasting colors, easy to apply (immersion or spraying), immediate color formation, and does not effect DNA. Disadvantages: may overspray, not specific protein dye, its use may require breathing apparatus.
Question 5 Place silicon cast between two small cardboard pieces. For dental stone casts use a druggist fold and place in a cardboard box.

Exercise P
Question 1 One may have to fabricate a larger box from two smaller boxes or may have to cut out or sample the evidence.

Question 2 Yes, as long as the evidence collector does the actual packaging and collection. This process promotes consistency.

Question 3 The evidence outer packaging is cut into at a location other than the sealed opening. Once the processing is completed then the new opening is sealed with tape and marked appropriately.

Question 4 The property list should include case number, item number, description of the item and packaging used, location at the crime scene, and time of collection.

Exercise Q

Question 1 Provided that all reconstruction activities at the scene are completed then after the final scene survey, the scene may be released.

Question 2 Reinitiate documentation through to collection at the scene.

Exercise R

Question 1 The medical examiner is responsible for identification of wounds, but a skilled and experienced crime scene investigator could give preliminary identifications to assist with reconstruction activities.

Question 2 The crime scene investigator must talk with the medical examiner and specifically address any omissions in the autopsy.

Exercise S

Question 1 It is not possible to determine the side from which force was applied if there are no pieces of glass still in place in the window frame. All other conclusions are guesses. A piece of glass with knowledge of which side was exterior or interior is needed.

Question 2 For 90-degree shots (straight-on) the holes will be round. All shots less than 90 degrees or more acute will be oval shaped.

Exercise T

Question 1 There are likely to be blood spatters on the suspect's clothes. Immediately photograph the spatters followed by careful preservation and collection of the clothes.

Question 2 Large caliber firearms will produce a larger amount of spatter. The further away the blood source is to the firearm will decrease the amount of high-force impact spatter present.

Question 3 Back-spatter will be produced in smaller amounts if there is forward spatter produced by a through and through wound.

Question 4 The secondary spatter could be confused with impact spatter by size comparisons, but it is usually present in smaller numbers. Secondary spatters will always be in close proximity to an increasing pool of blood.

Question 5 Yes, gravity will cause the spatter to curve downward on contact with the surface, which will produce an elongated stain with a false, more acute angle of impact. Determination of area of origin would then be too high.

Exercise V

Question 1 Range of Fire: loss of GSR on unknown targets and targets of known targets. Trajectory determinations: the careless placing of rods in the holes or by bumping or moving the rods around while in the holes may damage the holes. Ejection patterns: the ground may be hard causing casings to bounce or be easily moved. The shooter's hand position is highly variable from a normal upright shooting position (see Fig. V.6).

Question 2 Every time a firearm is used the mechanism becomes worn thusly creating unique firing abilities so that only the exact firearm must be used for the range-of-fire testing. The same ammunition must be used, as there may be differences between batches by the manufacturer. The number of known targets is determined by the amount of GSR present and the availability of ammunition.

Question 3 Lasers are effective at night. Visual trajectories are best during the day.

Question 4 A metal detector would help locate projectiles or casings at the crime scene.

Exercise W

Question 1 Following the suggested format.

Question 2 Using the evidence to determine what happened (gets easier with practice and experience).

Question 3 Not all the police reports are present, the autopsy report is missing, and all the lab test results are not given.

Index

experimentation of, 196, 197f
lasers in, 195f, 196
optical methods in, 196
strings in, 195f, 196
Transfer
   of bloodstain pattern, 172–173, 173f, 175f, 176–178
   direct, 13, 14f
   indirect, 13, 14f
   Locard Exchange Principle in, 13–18, 14f
Transient evidence, 139
   in preliminary scene survey, 31, 34
Transportation of evidence, 40
Triangulation, 70, 72
Tripod, 60f, 62, 65
Tunnel vision, 31
Tylenol, 116, 116t

U

Ultraviolet (UV) light, 90, 92t, 236
Urine, 102, 102f, 111

V

Vaginal fluid, 90, 92t
Victim
   description of, 40, 43–44
   first responders and, 235

gender of, 33
location of, 191, 199
statement of, 8
of victim, 33
Video placard, 49, 51, 52f
Videography, 49–54, 51f–52f, 240
Visualization
   of biological evidence, 97–108, 98f–100f, 171f–173f
   of chemical evidence, 109–120, 110t, 113t
   explosive residue tests in, 111–112, 111t, 114–116
   GSR tests in, 109–111, 110t
   heme-based reagents in, 98–100, 98f–99f, 103–104
   protein-reacting-based reagents in, 100, 100f, 104
   silicone casting in, 133, 134f

W

Weapons, note-taking and, 40, 43. *See also* Gunshot residue; Shooting investigation
Weather conditions, 31, 40, 42
Wheel method, 83–85, 83f
White light, 91, 93
Wipe pattern, 173

Witness
   first responders and, 21
   in multilevel security, 27
   physical evidence and, 8
   statement of, 8
Wound, 40, 43, 91, 236
Wound dynamics
   blunt force in, 154, 154t
   chemical burns in, 154, 154t
   in crime scene reconstruction, 153–154, 154t
   discussion questions on, 157, 242
   explosion in, 154, 154t
   laboratory exercise on, 155–157, 155f–157f
   types of, 154, 154t
Written record. *See* Note-taking

Y

Yellow barrier filter, 90–91, 92t

Z

Zinc, 110t
Zinc chloride, 115
Zirconium, 110t
Zone method, 83–85, 83f